PEER COUNSELING
AND
SELF-HELP GROUPS
ON CAMPUS

PEER COUNSELING AND SELF-HELP GROUPS ON CAMPUS

By

NORMAN S. GIDDAN, Ph.D.
Director, Counseling Center
University of Toledo
Toledo, Ohio

and

MICHAEL J. AUSTIN, Ph.D.
Director, Center for Social Welfare Research
School of Social Work
University of Washington
Seattle, Washington

KIRTLEY LIBRARY
COLUMBIA COLLEGE
COLUMBIA, MO 65216

CHARLES C THOMAS • PUBLISHER
Springfield • Illinois • U.S.A.

378.194
G36p

Published and Distributed Throughout the World by

CHARLES C THOMAS • PUBLISHER
2600 South First Street
Springfield, Illinois, 62717, U.S.A.

This book is protected by copyright. No part of it
may be reproduced in any manner without written
permission from the publisher.

© *1982 by* CHARLES C THOMAS • PUBLISHER

ISBN 0-398-04724-3

Library of Congress Catalog Card Number: 82-5875

With THOMAS BOOKS *careful attention is given to all details of
manufacturing and design. It is the Publisher's desire to present books that
are satisfactory as to their physical qualities and artistic possibilities and
appropriate for their particular use.* THOMAS BOOKS *will be true to those
laws of quality that assure a good name and good will.*

Printed in the United States of America

I-R5-1

Library of Congress Cataloging in Publication Data

Giddan, Norman S.
  Peer counseling and self-help groups on campus.

  Bibliography: p.
  Includes index.
  1. Peer group counseling of students—Case studies. 2. Self-
help groups—Case studies. I. Austin, Michael J. II. Title.
LB2343.G43   1982   378'.194   82-5875
ISBN 0-398-04724-3   AACR2

CONTRIBUTORS

Michael J. Austin, M.S.W., Ph.D.: Professor of Social Work and Director, Center for Social Welfare Research, University of Washington

Alexander Bassin, Ph.D.: Professor of Criminology, Florida State University

John R. Bonar, Ph.D.: Assistant Dean of Advising and Counseling; Research Associate, Career Education Center, Florida State University

Ernest T. Buchanan, III, J.D., Ph.D.: Professor and Dean, Tidewater Community College

Mary Burkhart, Ph.D.: Assistant Dean of Students, University of California at Irvine

Gary J. Faltico, Ph.D.: Director of Counseling, State University of New York at Purchase

Norman S. Giddan, Ph.D.: Professor and Director, University Counseling Center, University of Toledo

Barbara A. Jackson, M.S.: Counseling Center, Southwest Missouri State College

John Kalafat, Ph.D.: Director, Counseling Center, Farleigh Dickinson University

Harold A. Korn, Ph.D.: Professor of Psychology and Director, Counseling Services, University of Michigan

Carole S. Minor, M.S.: Assistant Director, Curricular-Career Information Service, Florida State University

Mary K. Price, Ph.D.: Career Education Center, Florida State University

Robert Reardon, Ph.D.: Professor of Education and Director, Curricular-Career Information Service, Florida State University

Donald L. Sanz, Ph.D.: Assistant Director, University Counseling Center, University of Toledo

Andi Schulman, B. A.: Coordinator of Training, Telephone Counseling Service, Florida State University

Michael B. Schwartz, D. S. W.: Professor of Psychiatry, Southern Illinois University Medical School

Mary P. Tyler, Ph.D.: Assistant Professor of Psychology, Florida State University

Julian Wohl, Ph.D.: Professor of Psychology, University of Toledo

FOREWORD

ANYONE interested in developing a peer counseling program in a college in the United States will have to give serious attention to *Peer Counseling and Self-Help Groups on Campus* by Norman Giddan and Michael Austin. This comprehensive book provides a remarkable overview of a variety of concrete programs, e.g. a telephone crisis counseling service, a campus drug information center, a career information service and so on. At the same time the book outlines in a down-to-earth, readable fashion the basic issues that surround such programs: training, evaluation, administrative authority.

The peer counseling movement that has been spreading rapidly at both the college and high school levels is particularly important in the present period when resources are tight and need is enormous. One of the important contributions of the self-help approach is the conversion of help seekers into problem solvers. The helpee becomes the helper and, in doing so, helps him or herself immeasurably.

The peer modality not only expands services quantitatively by creating a large number of service givers, but qualitatively as well since the service giver-receiver obtains new benefits from playing the help-giving role. Peer-peer relationships are less likely to produce dependence than the standard client-professional relationships. Finally, because the peer is nearer to the problem and shares it in an experiential fashion, he or she has access to another dimension of help. All of this, of course, is not to downgrade the role of the professional guidance counselor or psychologist who clearly has a complementary role to play in providing services and a series of new roles related to training the peers and monitoring or guiding the programs.

Peer Counseling and Self-help Groups on Campus

There is a host of evidence, beginning with Truax and including Brown and Delworth, that supports the effectiveness of nonprofessional helping. This book builds on that research providing new evidence and examples as well as very useful "how to" information. There is in addition a very useful cross-cultural perspective.

Frank Riessman
June, 1982

PREFACE

PEER Counseling and Self-help Groups on Campus is part of a growing body of evidence and thought that suggests that college students make excellent peer counselors, promoting their own adaptation to college in the context of helping others. The last fifteen years have seen the self-help and peer counseling movement link up with the needs and concerns of college communities. Self-help has obvious advantages for college students, since the social distance between helper and recipient is minimal. Experts feel that college students are among those who make the best volunteers, gain a great deal from it, and capitalize on a natural peer influence process that exists on campus.

The involvement of undergraduate or graduate students as peer counselors and organizers of self-help efforts on campus represents also a serious effort by mental health professionals to improve the quality and quantity of mental health services. New learning opportunities for students develop as well as supplements for the limited resources of professional staff. It is assumed that students can be quickly trained to acquire beginning counseling and community organizing skills to assist other students in adjusting to or changing an educational environment; easily developed or enhanced peer relationships predicated on the common status of the student role comprise the mediating process. The range of services includes crisis programs and telephone hot lines, outreach programs for freshmen and foreign students, educational advising, residence hall counseling, individual and group peer counseling, assertiveness training, program development, and self-help mental health groups.

This book presents innovative case studies in peer counseling and self-help practices, techniques and programs from a single college campus ... obvious kinship to similar wide-ranging programs at American University, Colorado State University and the University of South Florida. These case studies highlight the recruitment, selection, training, and supervision that characterize self-help and peer counseling at a majority of our universities. Each author, as a participant observer, describes the origins and early history of the program and its success based on surveys, interviews, and anecdotal records. Program descriptions together provide a model for planning and implementation on other campuses. The editors assisted in either the conception, implementation, or evaluation of these programs over a seven-year period.

The book begins with an introduction which places peer counseling programs within the context of the self-help and paraprofessional traditions in the human services. Section I on Counseling and Advising Strategies includes a crisis telephone counseling service, a career information service, a drug information service, an outreach service, and educational advising services. The needs and interests of particular groups, special settings, and difficult transitions or crises are emphasized. Section II on Self-help Strategies illustrates and describes women's discussion groups, residence hall self-help groups, self-help training for overseas counselors, a gay peer self-help program, and on-the-job learning as student administrative aides. The group is often important as the vehicle for training and helping process here, with simultaneous concern for individual help or service and social or environmental change. Section III includes a discussion of the implications and future directions of peer counseling and self-help by identifying legal, educational, and cross-cultural perspectives. It addresses interrelationships between liberal arts and experiential education, legal issues relevant to the work and role of paraprofessional counselors, and, last, we go across the Pacific Ocean in order to examine possibilities of peer counseling on Asian campuses. The final chapter, or Epilogue, ties together present trends and guidelines suggested by the program descriptions, with implications for adapting, evaluating, and extending such innovations elsewhere.

N. S. G.
M. J. A.

ACKNOWLEDGMENTS

THIS book emerged out of a unique combination of staff resources and administrative support at Florida State University. President J. Stanley Marshall and Dr. Stephen McClellan, Vice President of Student Affairs, actively encouraged the search for creative approaches to meeting the needs of college students. Dr. Harold A. Korn, Dean of Advising and Counseling, helped create the environment for implementing the innovative projects described in this volume.

Our typists provided generous help all along the way. Special thanks are due Janet Henderson, Coletta Lewandowski, Michelle Taylor Hudson, and Sandy Brown. We are very grateful to Millicent Shargel of Tallahassee for her superb editorial assistance. We also appreciate the efficient editorial work of William H. Bried at Charles C Thomas, Publisher.

Our wives, Jane and Sue, deserve much credit for their continuing support. We wish to recognize their contribution with our love and to dedicate this book to supportive spouses everywhere.

NSG
MJA

KIRTLEY LIBRARY
COLUMBIA COLLEGE
COLUMBIA, MO 65216

CONTENTS

Foreword. vii

Preface ix

Introduction: College Peer Counseling and Self-help Perspectives. 3

Section I. Counseling and Advising Strategies

Chapter

    1. Telephone Crisis Counseling Service — John Kalafat and Andi
       Schulman 27

    2. Curricular-Career Information Service — Robert Reardon,
       Carole S. Minor and Mary Burkhart 43

    3. A Campus Drug Information and Service Center — Alexander
       Bassin. 54

    4. An Academic Advising Service: Students Helping Students —
       John R. Bonar 65

    5. Project Alteract: A Student Designed Drop-in and Outreach
       Center — Norman S. Giddan, Donald L. Sanz, and Mary K.
       Price. 75

Section II. Self-help Strategies

    6. Organizing and Leading Women's Self-help Discussion
       Groups — Mary P. Tyler. 91

    7. Self-help Rap Groups and Peer Counseling in the Gay Com-
       munity — Michael B. Schwartz 104

    8. A Caring Community on Campus — Gary J. Faltico. 116

    9. Self-help Training of Student Counselors for Overseas
       Education Programs — Mary P. Tyler and Donald L. Sanz. 130

    10. Students as Administrative Aides: On-the-job Learning —
       Barbara A. Jackson 143

xiii

xiv *Peer Counseling and Self-help Groups on Campus*

Section III. Multiple Perspectives — Educational, Legal and Cross-cultural

11. Paraprofessionals and Issues of Legal Liability — Ernest T.
Buchanan, III. 155

12. Peer Counseling Viewed from a Cross-cultural Perspective —
Julian Wohl 161

13. Can Experiential Programs Help the Liberal Arts? — Harold A.
Korn 168

Epilogue: Implications for the Future. 174

Index 185

PEER COUNSELING
AND
SELF-HELP GROUPS
ON CAMPUS

INTRODUCTION:
College Peer Counseling and
Self-help Perspectives

PEER counseling programs are becoming important student services on college campuses where students are helping each other and themselves in many imaginative ways. Some students serve as career or academic counselors (Gadzella, 1979), working in lieu of professionals or alongside them, while others function as residence hall aides or student affairs staff orienting their fellow students to university life (Conroy, 1978). Hotlines and crisis centers increasingly rely on paraprofessional student personnel (Leventhal et al., 1976) and the same is true for women's centers, black studies programs, drug centers, reading and study skills centers, (Schauble and Resnick, 1976; Aiken et al., 1974; Allen, 1974).

Self-help groups have also appeared on campus in growing numbers in the last decade (Pierce and Schwartz, 1978; Sandmeyer et al., 1979; Barrow and Hetherington, 1981). Some have been concerned with women's liberation, gay rights, political campaigns, and tenants' rights. Katz and Bender (1976) characterize self-help groups as generally voluntary, involved with face-to-face interaction, spontaneously arising in an attempt to meet some need, solve a problem or achieve mutual benefits.

Self-help has become an important adjunct to professional and paraprofessional roles and in some cases has emerged as the result of an absence of professional interest and concern. During periods of crisis, trauma, or difficult transitions, the natural support systems have the potential to minimize disability or disturbance and promote the acquisition of new coping skills. The self-help process builds upon individual responsibility and perseverance by promoting mutual aid similar to the traditional "buddy" system. Self-help groups may also meet the important personal and social needs of affiliation and a sense of community. Both self-help groups and peer counseling and support programs seek to promote the ability of ordinary individuals to work together and resolve many of life's difficulties without professional intervention (Durman, 1976). Understanding the peer counseling and self-help movement on campus is not possible without at least a brief sketch of the historical antecedents of these processes in the fields of social welfare and mental health.

Historical Perspectives

The service of paraprofessionals or peer mental health workers can be traced back to the late eighteenth and early nineteenth century. Pinel (France), Tuke (England), and Benjamin Rush and Dorothea Lind Dix (America) developed a therapeutic philosophy and approach known as moral treatment, which is the first of the three mental health revolutions identified by Hobbs (1964). The second revolution, preoccupied with man's inner or intrapsychic life, was initiated by Sigmund Freud in Vienna. We participate in the third mental health revolution today, one which embraces a community approach to illness and mental health based on the principles of public health and human service (Sobey, 1970; Sauber, 1973) and goes beyond the medical model of the past few decades (Levine et al., 1979). Therapeutic methods of Carl Rogers and B. F. Skinner have assisted in the break with psychoanalytical approaches, contributing directly and indirectly to the paraprofessional movement by identifying principles for providing therapeutic assistance which can be specified, measured, and taught. Self-help programs are also tied to the philosophy and practice of the community mental health movement. As Dumont (1976, p. 126) has noted,

> The essence of the community mental health movement seemed to be that the gap between the people providing help and the people receiving help should not be so vast as more traditional mental health professionals thought necessary. The order and direction of that movement found a common path with the cultural and historical forces that led to the emergence of the self-help movement. Self-help programs

Introduction: College Peer Counseling and Self-help Perspectives 5

offered an alternative to the theoreticians of mental health care who took seriously the implications of social and community psychiatry.

Innovative social welfare legislation has also played a key role in the history of paraprofessionalism beginning in the 1930s with the Work's Progress Administration, Social Security Act of 1935, and National Youth Administration. Unemployed, out-of-school youth and potential drop-outs were recruited, given brief training, and placed as paraprofessionals in a number of social welfare fields. During the "War on Poverty" in the 1960s paraprofessionals worked in Youth Opportunity Centers, New Careers programs were concerned with entry level employment opportunities and career ladders, and additional federal legislation promoted the use of paraprofessionals in fields of juvenile delinquency and mental retardation. In 1961 the Joint Commission on Mental Illness and Health recommended the development of a national manpower recruitment and training program for professionals and on-the-job training for paraprofessionals.

Last, we might mention the political power and control of professionals which have been under attack by self-help and paraprofessionalism as forces to counteract the power of professionalism (Dumont, 1976). At its best the self-help movement brings the community into the planning, the design, and the actual implementation of service programs.

The rich heritage of the self-help movement has been well documented elsewhere by Katz and Bender (1976), Killilea (1976), and Dumont (1976). The history of mutual aid and mutual help forcefully demonstrates that humans are social beings who must satisfy their own needs while at the same time they must cooperate with each other in order to survive and adapt.

Utopian communities and the trade unions are clear examples of mutual aid in contemporary United States history. The union self-help approach was extended to wages, benefits, child labor laws and the education of its workers. Throughout history, people have needed help, support, solace and cooperation from fellow human beings. The American tradition of self-help can be seen in the origins of Alcoholics Anonymous, which began in the Oxford Group's (later known as Moral Rearmament) "open confession" within large groups of college students. A. A. is further related to the American Protestant tradition and the pragmatic philosophies of William James and John Dewey.

The Characteristics of Self-help

Self-help groups have multiple functions and characteristics. The personal participation of each member helps to build relationships and provide a reference point for individuals; purposes for coming together vary but it is usually from a position of powerlessness (Katz and Bender, 1976). Among the most well-known self-help groups in society are Alcoholics Anonymous, Synanon, Parents Without Partners, Widow-to-Widow, and the Association of Retarded Citizens. Such groups meet needs which are unfulfilled, provide alternative service, and promote a sense of affiliation and community (Lieberman and Borman, 1976). Self-help is seen as contributing to a kind of dual revolution, one that enhances individual social competence and relationships while simultaneously affecting society's attitudes and institutions.

Levy's (1976) survey of self-help groups found considerable variability among and within groups. The membership of many self-help groups cuts across lines of social class and ethnicity. Except for Alcoholics Anonymous, he found that most groups were predominantly females. Striving for an integrative theory of intervention, he developed a set of behavioral and cognitive dimensions, noted in Table I, which encompass the psychological, social, and cultural processes of self-help groups.

This set of processes has parallels in Gartner and Riessman's (1977) description of how self-help works. They, too, emphasize peer support, encouragement and reinforcement, and self-reinforcement obtained while helping. While Levy (1976) stressed training, suggestion, and modeling as processes to assist with behavior and environmental change, Gartner and Riessman (1977) emphasized the group member as comprising a vital and unique role, both as a social change agent and as a consumer advocate, where ideology goes beyond the needs of the individual to the larger society and a commitment for social justice and change.

Both approaches to the self-help process limit themselves to group process and the various involvements and activities of the members or consumers, and each emphasize, albeit differently,

Introduction: College Peer Counseling and Self-help Perspectives 7

the helper-therapy principle. This principle stipulates that the helper may grow and change as much, often more, than the individual being helped. Neither approach to self-help pays a great deal of attention to psychological insight or the expression of feeling and emotion.

Table I

PROCESSES OF SELF-HELP GROUPS

Behavioral Focus

1. Both direct and vicarious social reinforcement for the development of ego-syntonic behavior and the elimination of problematic behavior.
2. Training, indoctrination, and support in the use of various kinds of self-control behavior.
3. Modeling of methods of coping with stresses and changing behavior.
4. Providing members with an agenda of (and rationale for) actions they can engage in to change their social environment.

Cognitive Focus

1. Providing members with a rationale for their problems or distress, and for the group's way of dealing with it, thereby removing their mystification over their experiences and increasing their expectancy for change and help.
2. Provision of normative and instrumental information and advice.
3. Expansion of the range of alternative perceptions of members' problems and circumstances and of actions that they might take to cope with their problems.
4. Enhancement of members' discriminative abilities regarding the stimulus and event contingencies in their lives.
5. Support for changes in attitudes towards one's self, one's own behavior, and society.
6. Reduction or elimination of a sense of isolation or uniqueness regarding members' problems and experiences through the operation of social comparison and consensual validation.
7. The development of an alternative or substitute culture and social structure within which members can develop new definitions of their personal identities and new norms upon which they can base their self-esteem.

One important difference is that Gartner and Riessman stress the so-called "aprofessional dimension" in contrasting the professional and nonprofessional modes of human service. The nonprofessional orientation is seen as more flexible, more activist, more concrete use of common sense, and more spontaneous than the professional approach to helping. Gartner and Riessman (1977) see the flexibility as critical in assisting self-helpers in relating to each other's world views and expectations. Some other features of the self-help process (Killilea, 1976; Schwartz, 1971) include reference group identification, mutual support and peer communication, honesty and lowered defenses, strict group discipline and limit setting, collective belief and blind faith, family atmosphere without an authority figure, and the closeness to reality brought about through constructive action toward shared goals.

There are dangers inherent in some of the self-help movement ideology. For example, paraprofessionals may assist a teacher or a professional, but may also oppose the essence of the teaching or helping process. For some, the self-help philosophy has led to a simplistic anti-professional and anti-intellectual orthodoxy. Self-help may also promote too much dependency for too long by exacerbating problems such as

> ... the unequal and unjust distribution of resources and power within our society, the fragmentation of our communities, the tendency to blame the victim rather than changing the victimizing circumstance, the advancing medicalization of all aspects of human life, and the increasing ascendancy of technology over caring within our professional human services. (Sidel and Sidel, 1976, p. 67)

Gartner and Riessman (1977) warn that participants in self-help groups may get caught up in a momentary crisis, lose perspective and balance. The group process can be used defensively, as a vehicle for self-deception, and avoidance of personal responsibility and constructive change may result.

The self-help approaches related to personal growth, social advocacy, creating alternative life-styles, or survival as an outcast (Katz and Bender, 1976) have obvious and natural advantages for college students, too. Most experts feel that college students make the best volunteers and gain a great deal from it. The social distance between helper and recipient is minimal since students share characteristics like age, experience, goals, and developmental status. Students are often in flux while actually living in an institution committed to active development. When students engage in self-help, they capitalize on the natural peer influence process which permeates the campus. Dormitory bull sessions, the long, heated discussions over beer and coffee, students endlessly talking about themselves and learning from others — these experiences

Introduction: College Peer Counseling and Self-help Perspectives 9

help shape identities and reflect vital developmental processes that peer counseling and self-help are built upon. College peer counselors gain confidence and flexibility, assertiveness and understanding, and tolerance and empathy (Gruver, 1971).

DEFINING THE PARAPROFESSIONALS' ROLES OF CAMPUS PEER COUNSELORS

It is difficult to be precise or reach agreement about what constitutes a paraprofessional. The term is used to designate a peer counselor, aide, support personnel, mental health worker, volunteer, paramedic, para-legal, and so many others (Zimpfer, 1974). The widely acclaimed model of student paraprofessionals for higher education of Delworth et al. (1974) defines a paraprofessional as a person without extended professional training who is specifically selected, trained, and given on-going supervision to perform some designated portion of the tasks usually performed by the professional. Additionally, the paraprofessional is involved primarily with agency activities, works in an area limited by specific skills, is usually a member of the population being served, and generally receives some form of remuneration.

By contrasting the original New Careers roles with those of the typical peer counselors we may see the "intent" behind each. New Careerists were to be selected from the "indigenous" population served, thus share the cultural background, mores, socioeconomic status, language and values of the clients. Permanent jobs, adequate compensation and the building of an upwardly mobile career system were part of the intent of this development. It contrasts sharply with the model of the more-or-less transient student volunteer. Such students may or may not receive formal training, often receive only academic credit and usually stay in a program anywhere from six months to two years. Participation often leads to important personal or career growth, but it is not the intent of the program to create permanent jobs.

Brammer (1977) distinguishes between paraprofessionals and professionals by emphasizing each group may be able to provide specific kinds of helping services under certain conditions. Professionals have a range of skills in research, a wide theoretical vista allowing them to conceptualize their activities, formal ethical commitments to professional codes, professional peer surveillance and that hard-to-define "clinical judgment factor." He further refines the professional versus paraprofessional controversy by distinguishing two other categories of human services workers — the volunteer and the "indigenous peer helper." While definitions are still inconclusive, it is important to account for the complexities of tasks, roles, competence, educational level, background, job permanence, career mobility, and recent developments in theory and practice in specifying professional and paraprofessional roles. Some of the key roles assumed by paraprofessionals are:

1. *Aide:* Past tasks were menial and routine, but today's functions cover an extensive range of activities, such as the newer social relationship therapies.
2. *Bridge:* The indigenous nonprofessional serves as a bridge between the middle-class professional and the consumer, often different in age, ethnic group and life-style (Reiff and Reissman, 1970).
3. *Agent of Change:* The paraprofessional can bring about the integration of community services; stress activity and direct, concrete, aggressive problem-solving.
4. *The Expediter:* The use of paraprofessionals permits the coordination of services without loss of autonomy for the various agencies involved.

Many of the problems that manifest themselves in programs utilizing paraprofessionals have their origin in the lack of clarity over roles, identity, and expectations. Unrealistic expectations, from whatever source, may discourage the conscientious paraprofessional (Eisdorfer and Golann, 1969; Ishiyama, McCulley, and Rodriguez, 1967).

PROGRAM IMPACT AND EVALUATION

Issues concerned with the paraprofessional and self-help approach are quite complex, interrelated and not easily resolved. The most critical issues are those surrounding the paraprofessional role, status, performance, benefits, training and supportive services. Several authorities have also made recommendations and developed guidelines that may be applied to paraprofessional college

Introduction: College Peer Counseling and Self-help Perspectives

Table II

KEY ISSUES RELATED TO PARAPROFESSIONALISM AND SELF-HELP

1. *Paraprofessionals have not produced uniform efficient, effective services nor have they radically changed service delivery systems and organizations.* There has been a great deal of professional and agency resistance to the introduction of paraprofessionals. Professionals have refused to work with them, or been unwilling to adopt the required roles of training, consultation and supervision. Even in the face of supportive data and evidence to the contrary, the argument still goes that paraprofessionals have not produced an increase in service efficiency, nor been a force for change in an agency. How reasonable was such an original set of expectations?

2. *Paraprofessionals have been exploited personally, vocationally and financially.* This set of issues focuses upon inherent job limitations and the lack of career mobility. Trained paraprofessionals who are evaluated for "life experiences" have usually not translated their skills into job-relevant terminology for use in the job market and career mobility. Compensation and status may be diminished since they are set by credentials, not by a more objective set of criteria or "standards for work."

3. *A number of factors have constrained or hurt the performance of paraprofessionals including real-world limitations.* The lack of a college degree and other credentials obviously hurts in this society, as does the orientation toward technical and medical "experts."

4. *Many factors are involved in administering an effective paraprofessional service.* In addition to the adoption of realistic expectations about the capacities of paraprofessionals, it is important to have solid administrative leadership, commitment, adequate funding, and appropriate, well-located physical facilities for successful paraprofessional programs.

5. *Paraprofessionals should have opportunities to advance themselves.* It is important that job, academic degree, and inservice training opportunities be connected to increasing levels of expectation. The legal rights and obligations of paraprofessionals in various levels and in different positions should be established. Any fair concept of adequate compensation would establish equal pay for equivalent, if not also comparable, work.

6. *Coordination and cooperation among colleges, job-related training and job market availability must be established nationwide.* Universities must open themselves to paraprofessional training and programs, more nontraditional learning. Such training programs might help universities change, and to widen the horizon of their curriculum. Jobs must be available that are linked specifically to the output of training and higher education degree programs. Life experience, natural ability, and on-the-job training must be properly evaluated in terms of their relationships to job performance and job competence.

7. *Steps should be taken by programs and agencies to enhance paraprofessional effectiveness.* Both paraprofessionals and professionals must receive the training that new roles require. All constituencies involved in program planning, namely, the community, the target audience, paraprofessionals and professionals should be contacted when there are problems to be solved or programs to be planned.

and community programs (Delworth, 1974; Delworth et al., 1974; Alley et al., 1979; Pearl, 1974, 1981; Wagenfeld and Robin, 1981; Gartner and Riessman, 1974; Kahn, et al., 1981). A compressed overview of key issues and recommendations related to paraprofessionalism and self-help are summarized in Table II.

In addition to the identification of key issues, programs need to be examined in terms of the steps, processes and procedures used to develop paraprofessional activities. Delworth et al., (1974) have identified the following features of successful campus programs, but they also apply to hospital, agency and community efforts.

1. Assessment: Program needs must be established with sufficient administrative support, resources and benefits to the college, the program and the paraprofessionals.
2. Planning and organization: Specific and clear job descriptions, sufficient clerical staff and funding are necessary.
3. Selection of paraprofessionals: Recruitment procedures must be established and qualifications for the positions set up.
4. Selection of professionals: Professionals working with paraprofessionals should be interested, secure and skilled.
5. Training: It is recommended that there be both core and specific training components. Generalized skills are required, usually, as well as skills specific to the particular school, agency and task involved.
6. Evaluation: This ensures feedback to the staff that goals are being met and may provide data supporting program continuation and credibility.

There are now more than 3,000 articles, books, reports, experiments and testimonials concerned with paraprofessionals, peer counseling and self-help groups (Scott and Warner, 1974; Zimpfer, 1974; Cowen, 1973; Gershon and Biller, 1977). Even though subjective impressions by either the program developers or the participants have been complemented by more rigorous quasi-experimental evaluations, the evidence is still largely favorable to paraprofessional counseling. There is widespread agreement that under some circumstances certain kinds of people can be

Introduction: College Peer Counseling and Self-help Perspectives 13

trained rather quickly to help other individuals (Gruver, 1971; Brown, 1974; Karlsruher, 1974; Durlak, 1973; Hoffman and Warner, 1976). Peer counseling appears to be most substantiated in efforts to promote academic adjustment and educational support. The major disputes now seem to center on how well paraprofessional counseling works, how widely it can be used and with what kinds of populations, and establishing the principal parameters of training and supervision. Moreover, variables such as age, sex, socioeconomic status, and degree of client-counselor similarity need to be related to peer counseling process and outcome.

Part of the explanation for the effectiveness of paraprofessional peer counselors is that they share the characteristics of language, values, customs, personality, and life-style with their clients or consumers. Resistance is broken down through these kinds of similarities and shared identifications, and it is thought that the peer counselor is better able to understand, to be compassionate, and to be more empathic with similar individuals. Studies are now appearing, though, which question this assumption of shared attitudes or life-styles leading to enhanced empathy and, in turn, to more client change and growth (Taylor, 1974; Andrade and Burstein, 1978).

Assessments of self-help groups and peer counseling programs have not been conducted with sound quasi-experimental methodology, although some studies using pre- and post-measures, control groups, objective criteria and appropriate statistical techniques do exist according to Gershon and Biller (1977). Unfortunately, many of the methodological, statistical and design problems that generally plague the psychotherapy process and outcome research are found here, too. There is also a need for careful cost-effectiveness and cost-benefit research (Haskell, 1981).

The last evaluation issue relates to staff mix in terms of the numbers and types of professionals and paraprofessionals. It is generally presumed that the paraprofessional, even if paid fairly, will be less costly than professionals and that costs for selection, training and supervision are not sufficient to outweigh the salary savings. Marschak and Henke (1979) have calculated the hourly services of professionals and paraprofessionals, and taken into account average productivity. Their models are built upon the variables of staff hours, usage by patients and salary levels; but quality of service, benefits to client, freeing professionals for other duties, and translation of service into financial terms remain issues to be resolved. While they note that paraprofessionals contribute significantly to the output as measured, their productivity in a mental health center depends on the way that they are used in the center and on the characteristics of the center's client population. This approach may be promising for trying to find staffing ratios that will facilitate paraprofessional-professional cooperation and efficiency. Quality of service and client benefits also need to be included in such models.

College students first served as paraprofessional counselors or therapeutic agents in Companion Programs in mental hospitals, originated at Metropolitan State Hospital in 1954 by Harvard University. Students still serve in hospital settings (Scheibe et al., 1969; Rappaport et al., 1971), but their efforts have spread to guidance clinics, school settings, troubled children and adolescents (Cowen et al., 1966; Stollak, 1969), and more recently to the campus community and community mental health (Bloom, 1975; Nash et al., 1978). Some of the difficulties that have plagued New Careers and inner city paraprofessional programs are not as troublesome or frequent in campus settings. The student role as peer counselor is more or less for the period of college attendance, so there is no need for a permanent career ladder or lattice for any given individual. Second, since proposed changes in campus agencies or administrative structure are usually minor, such programs do not risk the resistance that has been found when more profound structural and social change has been attempted in the community. Third, professional claims tend to be weak, ambiguous or absent in many of the areas into which peer counseling has developed on campus which according to Wagenfeld and Robin (1981) should reduce competition and promote success.

A recent review of undergraduate paraprofessionals identified the following personal characteristics as desirable for undergraduate peer counselors (German, 1979): (1) a genuine desire to contribute to the social and personal development of others; (2) good communication skills; (3) ability to create an emotional climate leading to growth; (4) sound personal adjustment; (5) a capacity to manage one's own school life successfully; (6) leadership skills;

Introduction: College Peer Counseling and Self-help Perspectives 15

and (7) the capacity to profit from training and supervision. No single selection procedure seems to work in all programs and on all campuses.

Gruver (1971) suggests some of the potential disadvantages or problems that may arise in using naive college students in therapeutic or quasi-therapeutic roles. There may be a projection of student difficulties on to those whom he or she is supposed to help, burdening the helpees with one's own problems. Some students may try to "play" at being a professional therapist or else try and exploit their fellow students in some other way. It is also possible to shoot for a "peak experience" knowing that future responsibility may not have to be dealt with as one is only a student for a fixed period of time. Some students may think they have nothing to lose since there is no professional status or position that is at risk. Careful recruitment, selection, and training may help address these issues.

Students generally prefer to seek out other students for help with personal and social concerns. They like peer counselors of similar age and socioeconomic background, and race is important to minorities (Smith, 1974). Peer relationships are usually an important source of gratification, of learning about the self and relationships, and a principle mechanism by which identity is confirmed. Several basic directions have characterized peer counseling on campus, but the first and foremost is still academic information or support and educational adjustment counseling. A classic, unchallenged study by Zunker and Brown (1966) on academic counseling received by students from both professionals and trained student counselors found that entering freshmen who were oriented by students acquired and retained more information than those advised by professionals. The advising activities included survival orientation, test interpretation, study habits guidance, and a study skills survey.

IMPLICATIONS FOR THE FUTURE

Higher Education

The paraprofessional revolution has raised questions about the relevance of the traditional liberal arts curriculum, the need to update teaching techniques, and the value of experiential learning (Christmas et al., 1970; Persons et al., 1973; Harvey and Passy, 1981). Competency-based university programs can serve as innovative mechanisms for evaluating the professional and paraprofessional performance.

Campus counseling services are also in need of renovation (Morrill and Oetting, 1970; Banning and Aulepp, 1971; Steenland, 1973; Crane et al., 1975; Bloom, 1970). An integration of the scattered and varied campus counseling services could lead to more meaningful research and a comprehensive multi-service center approach characterized by: linkage with relevant academic departments (psychology, counseling, social work); cooperative endeavors by collecting and disseminating information; leadership in organizing and facilitating the efforts of varied departments; assessment of campus climate, development of services, training of both professionals and paraprofessionals, consultation and educational services; the conduct of research and program evaluation; and the creation of task forces and teams representing relevant disciplines, and university staff and students directed at improving the educational environment on campuses. Paraprofessionals and self-help groups could develop new roles in such an integrative resource network (Delworth and Hanson, 1980; Morrill and Hurst, 1980; Sarason et al., 1977).

Professionalism

The professional associations have come to take the paraprofessional revolution seriously, reflecting a freer, more flexible and constructive attitude toward the whole issue of levels and patterns of staffing. Ralph Simon (1970) originally called for the American Psychological Association and the National Association of Social Workers to come together and work jointly on the issue of the paraprofessional. The American Personnel and Guidance Association (APGA Sub-Committee on Support Personnel, 1967) early adopted statements which were guardedly favorable toward the use of paraprofessionals. The American Psychological Association (Korman, 1974) made mention of a "psychological service orientation" at varied levels with different objectives needing or reflecting diverse skills. This position statement also spoke of

Introduction: College Peer Counseling and Self-help Perspectives 17

career lattices and of bringing social relevance and multi-cultural considerations into psychological training. Speaking of Associates of Art graduates, it suggested that the science of psychology develop "a means for affiliation under the overall APA umbrella." Even opposition to the nonprofessionals or to self-help may now take the form of requests for more research, and a desire for better understanding of what works and why.

Natural Counseling

The cumulative weight of the evidence, however presumptive, suggests that peer counseling and self-help approaches are effective and efficient (Brown, 1974; Durlak, 1973; Karlsruher, 1974; Hoffman and Warner, 1976). Drug addicts, hospitalized chronic schizophrenics, college students, and stigmatized minority groups, such as gays, have all accomplished goals through a variety of new programs and services. The fact that ex-prisoners or ex-alcoholics may make the best helper under some circumstances may still surprise a few professionals and many in the community.

A natural style of counseling and therapy seems to be gradually emerging (Hurvitz, 1974) in which one can be openly judgmental, revealing and loving at times with clients and peers, yet where groups set very strict norms and mores with which the individual must synchronize. Emphasis is given to caring and change in the "here and now." In most self-help groups there is very little exploration of interpersonal dynamics, seldom a give-and-take among group members designed to work out their own particular relationships (Levy, 1976). In the typical women's discussion group, as an example, there may be much concern with women's relationships with their mothers, their aunts, and their friends outside the group, but there is decidedly little emphasis on the working out of interpersonal nuances among and between the women participants. Some natural counseling approaches borrow heavily from encounter groups, too, where there may be a lot of pressure put on an individual, including guilt, hostility, and shame actively evoked and manipulated. But lessened personal and social distance, and increased felt sharing and involvement are the real hallmarks of professionalism, according to Abrahms (1976).

Conclusion

The honeymoon is over in paraprofessionalism and soon will be for self-help groups as well. Pressures from the community helped originally to promote the paraprofessional approach based on very little evidence, but paraprofessionals have been caught in the cut-backs and economic insecurity of the times. Ph.D. and Master's level professionals are now filling their slots. Correspondingly, legal boundaries are not clear, ethical sanctions for paraprofessionals are uncertain, and they do not have the vocational identification that characterizes the professional. Woody (1976) suggests that they must now earn the respectability that they so much want as a group. they must handle their service or employment not only with responsibility but with a commitment to acquire the relevant knowledge, facts and techniques that they need, as well as the personal qualities that will enhance their roles. In the same spirit, Grzegorek (1976) reviews the current status of paraprofessional services and reminds us that there is no short-cut method to achieve community acceptance, support, and lastingness.

Prospects for some political and social change through self-help groups seem promising, even if some groups utilize single-issue political strategies. There is an emerging blend of mutual peer support, political consciousness-raising, and community change. There are those (Pearl, 1981) who feel that our inadequate and unfair social, political, and economic systems preclude paraprofessionals and self-helpers from succeeding. But the general community and the campus community recognize that paraprofessional services and self-help activities can support, encourage, and bolster persons in need as well as promote significant community change. (James, 1979).

REFERENCES

Abrahams, R. B. Mutual helping: Styles of caregiving in a mutual aid program—The Widowed Service Line. Chapter 11 in Caplan, G., & Killilea, M. (Eds.), *Support systems and mutual help: Multidisciplinary explorations.* New York: Grune & Stratton, 1976.

Aiken, J., Brownell, A., & Iscoe, I. The training and utilization of paraprofessionals in a college psychological service center. *Journal of College Student Personnel,* 1974, *15,* 480-486.

Introduction: College Peer Counseling and Self-help Perspectives   19

Allen, E. E. Paraprofessionals in a large-scale university program. *Personnel and Guidance Journal,* 1974, *53,* 281-284.

Alley, S., Blanton, J., Feldman, R. E., Hunter, G. D., & Rofson, M. *Case studies of mental health paraprofessionals.* New York: Human Sciences Press, 1979.

Andrade, S. J., & Burstein, A. G. Social congruence and empathy in parapro- fessional and professional mental health workers. Chapter 9 (III) in Nash, K. B., Jr., Lifton, N., & Smith, S. E. (Eds.), *The paraprofessional: Se- lected readings.* New Haven: Advocate Press, 1978.

Banning, J. H., & Aulepp, L. A. Staffing patterns of campus mental health facilities in the west: Monograph No. 2. *Improving mental health ser- vices on western campuses.* Boulder, Colo.: Western Interstate Com- mission for Higher Education, April 1971.

Barrow, J., & Hetherington, C. Training paraprofessionals to lead social- anxiety management groups. *Journal of College Student Personnel,* 1981, *22,* 269-273.

Bloom, B. L. Current issues in the provision of campus community mental health services. *Journal of the American College Health Association,* 1970, *18,* 257-264.

Bloom, B. L. (Ed.). *Psychological stress in the campus community: Theory, research and practice.* New York: Behavioral Publications, 1975.

Brammer, L. M. Who can be a helper? *Personnel and Guidance Journal,* 1977, *55*(6), 303-308.

Brown, W. F. Effectiveness of paraprofessionals: The evidence. *Personnel and Guidance Journal,* 1974, *53,* 257-263.

Christmas, J. J., Wallace, H., & Edwards, J. New careers and new mental health services: Fantasy or future? *American Journal of Psychiatry,* 1970, *126,* 1480-1486.

Conroy, J. K. Paid student paraprofessionals. *National Association of Stu- dent Personnel Administrators Journal,* 1978, *15*(3), 18-24.

Cowen, E. L. Social and community interventions. In Mussen, P., & Ro- senzweig, M. (Eds.), *Annual Review of Psychology,* 1973, *24,* 423-472.

Cowen, E. L., Zax, M., & Laird, J. D. A college student volunteer program in the elementary school setting. *Community Mental Health Journal,* 1966, *2,* 319-328.

Crane, J., Anderson, W., & Kirchner, K. Counseling center directors' attitudes toward paraprofessionals. *Journal of College Student Personnel,* 1975, *16*(2), 119-122.

Delworth, U. Paraprofessionals as guerrilas: Recommendations for system change. *Personnel and Guidance Journal,* *53,* 1974, 335-338.

Delworth, U., & Hanson, G. R. (Eds.). *Student services − A handbook for the profession.* San Francisco: Jossey-Bass, 1980.

Delworth, U., Sherwood, G., & Casaburri, N. *Student paraprofessionals: A working model for higher education.* Student Personnel Series No. 17. Washington, D.C.: American Personnel and Guidance Association, 1974.

Dumont, M. P. Self-help treatment programs. Chapter 4 in Caplan, G., & Killilea, M. (Eds.). *Support systems and mutual help: Multidisciplinary explorations.* New York: Grune & Stratton, 1976.

Durlak, J. A. Myths concerning the nonprofessional therapist. *Professional Psychology,* 1973, *4,* 300-304.

Durman, E. C. The role of self-help in service provision. *Journal of Applied Behavioral Science,* 1976, *12*(3), 433-443.

Eisdorfer, C., & Golann, S. E. Principles for the training of "New Professionals" in mental health. *Community Mental Health Journal,* 1969, *5,* 349-357.

Gadzella, B. M. The effects of student-to-student counseling on students' perceptions of study habits and attitudes. *Journal of College Student Personnel,* 1979, *20,* 424-430.

Gartner, A., & Riessman, F. *Self-help in the human services.* San Francisco: Jossey-Bass, 1977.

Gartner, A., & Riessman, F. The paraprofessional movement in perspective. *Personnel and Guidance Journal,* 1974, *53,* 253-256.

German, S. C. Selecting undergraduate paraprofessionals on college campuses: A review. *Journal of College Student Personnel,* 1979, *20,* 28-34.

Gershon, M., & Biller, H. B. *The other helpers.* Lexington, Mass.: D. C. Heath, 1977.

Gruver, G. G. College students as therapeutic agents. *Psychological Bulletin,* 1971, *76,* 111-127.

Grzegorek, A. E. On the status of paraprofessional services. Chapter in Schauble, P. G., & Resnick, J. L. (Eds.), *Paraprofessional training: Functions, methods and issues.* Volume II. Psychological and Vocational Counseling Center Monograph Series. Psychological and Vocational Counseling Center and Division of Continuing Education, University of Florida, 1976.

Harvey, M. R., & Passy, L. E. A university-based new careers program. Chapter III in Robin, S. S., & Wagenfeld, M. O. (Eds.), *Paraprofessionals in the human services.* New York: Human Sciences Press, 1981.

Haskell, M. A. The economics of paraprofessional employment. Chapter 3 (I) in Robin, S. S., & Wagenfeld, M. O. (Eds.), *Paraprofessionals in the human services.* New York: Human Sciences Press, 1981.

Hobbs, N. Mental health's third revolution. *The American Journal of Orthopsychiatry,* 1964, *36,* 822-833.

Hoffman, A. M., & Warner, R. W., Jr. Paraprofessional effectiveness. *Personnel and Guidance Journal,* 1976, *54,* 494-497.

Hurvitz, N. Similarities and differences between conventional psychotherapy and peer self-help psychotherapy groups. In Roman, P. S., & Price, H. M. (Eds.), *The sociology of psychotherapy.* New York: Aranson, 1974.

Ishiyama, T., McCulley, W., & Rodriguez, O. Does the psychiatric aide have a treatment role? *Mental Hygiene.* 1967, *51,* 115-118.

Introduction: College Peer Counseling and Self-help Perspectives   21

James, V. Paraprofessionals in mental health: A framework for the facts. Chapter 1 (I) in Alley, S. R., Blanton, J., & Feldman, R. E. (Eds.), *Paraprofessionals in mental health.* New York: Human Sciences Press, 1979.

Kahn, M. W., Henry, J., & Lejero, L. Indigenous mental health paraprofessionals on an Indian reservation. Chapter III in Robin, S. S., & Wagenfeld, M. O. (Eds.), *Paraprofessionals in the human services.* New York: Human Sciences Press, 1981.

Karlsruher, A. E. The nonprofessional as a psychotherapeutic agent. *American Journal of Community Psychology,* 1974, *2,* 61-77.

Katz, A. H., & Bender, E. I. (Eds.) *The strength in us.* New York: Franklin Watts, 1976.

Killilea, M. Mutual help organizations: Interpretations in the literature. Chapter 2 in Caplan, G., & Killilea, M. (Eds.), *Support systems and mutual help: Multidisciplinary explorations.* New York: Grune & Stratton, 1976.

Korman, M. National conference on levels and patterns of professional training in psychology: The major themes. *American Psychologist,* 1974, *29,* 441-449.

Leventhal, A. M., Berman, A. L., McCarthy, B. W., & Wasserman, C. W. Peer counseling on the university campus. *Journal of College Student Personnel,* 1976, *17,* 504-509.

Levine, M., Tulkin, S., Intagliata, J., Perry, J., & Whitson, E. The paraprofessional: A brief social history. Chapter 2 (I) in Alley, S.R., Blanton, J., & Feldman, R. E. (Eds.), *Paraprofesionals in mental health.* New York: Human Sciences Press, 1979.

Levy, L. H. Self-help groups: Types and psychological processes. *Journal of Applied Behavioral Science,* 1976, *12* (3), 310-322.

Lieberman, M. A., & Borman, L. D. Self-help and social research. *Journal of Applied Behavioral Science,* 1976, *12* (3), 455-463.

Marschak, T., & Henke, C. Achieving economic efficiency with paraprofessionals. Chapter 3 (II) in Alley, S. R., Blanton, J., & Feldman, R. E. (Eds.), *Paraprofessionals in mental health.* New York: Human Sciences Press, 1979.

Morrill, W. H., & Hurst, J. C. (Eds.). *Dimensions of intervention for student development.* New York: John Wiley & Sons, 1980.

Morrill, W. H. & Oetting, E. R. Outreach programs in college counseling. *Journal of College Student Personnel,* 1970, *11,* 50-53.

Nash, K. B., Jr., Lifton, N., & Smith, S. E. (Eds.). *The paraprofessional: Selected readings.* New Haven: Advocate Press, 1978.

Pearl, A. The paraprofessional in human service. Chapter I in Robin, S. S., & Wagenfeld, M. O. (Eds.). *Paraprofessionals in the human services.* New York: Human Sciences Press, 1981.

Pearl, A. Paraprofessionals and social change. *Personnel and Guidance Journal,* 1974, *53,* 264-268.

22   *Peer Counseling and Self-help Groups on Campus*

Persons, R. W., Clark, C., Persons, M., Kadish, M., & Patterson, W. Training and employing undergraduates as therapists in a college counseling service. *Professional Psychology,* 1973, *4,* 170-186.

Pierce, R. A., & Schwartz, A. J. Student self-help groups in a college mental health program. *Journal of College Student Personnel,* 1978, *19*(4), 321-324.

Rappaport, J., Chinsky, J. M., & Cowen, E. L. *Innovations in helping chronic patients: College students in a mental institution.* New York: Academic Press, 1971.

Reiff, R., & Riessman, F. The indigenous nonprofessional: A strategy of change in community action and community mental health programs. *Community Mental Health Journal Monograph Series,* No. 1 (4th printing). New York: Behavioral Publications, 1970.

Sandmeyer, L. E., Ranck, A. W., & Chiswick, N. R. A peer assertiveness-training program. *Personnel and Guidance Journal,* 1979, *57,* 304-306.

Sarason, S. B., Carroll, C., Maton, K., Cohen, S., & Lorentz, E. *Human services and resources networks.* San Francisco: Jossey-Bass, 1977.

Sauber, S. R. *Preventive educational intervention for mental health.* Cambridge: Ballinger, 1973.

Schauble, P. G., & Resnick, J. L. *Paraprofessional training: Functions, methods, and issues.* Volume II. Psychological and Vocational Counseling Center Monograph Series. Psychological and Vocational Counseling Center and Division of Continuing Education, University of Florida, 1976.

Scheibe, K. E., Kulik, J. A., Hirsch, P. D., & La Mocchia, S. *College students on chronic wards.* New York: Behavioral Publications, 1969.

Schwartz, E. K. Self-help organizations: Lessons to be learned for community psychology. Chapter in Milman, D. S., & Goldman, G. D. (Eds.), *Psychoanalytic contributions to community psychology.* Springfield, Ill.: Charles C Thomas, Publisher, 1971.

Scott, S. H., & Warner, R. W., Jr. Peer counseling. *Personnel and Guidance Journal,* 1974, *53,* 228-234.

Sidel, V. W., & Sidel, R. Beyond coping. *Social Policy,* 1976, *7*(2), 67-69.

Simon, R. The paraprofessionals are coming! The paraprofessionals are coming! American Psychological Association Convention, September 1970, Miami, Florida.

Smith, D. Preferences of university students for counselors and counseling settings. *Journal of College Student Personnel,* 1974, *15,* 53-57.

Sobey, F. *The nonprofessional revolution in mental health.* New York: Columbia University Press, 1970.

Steenland, R. Paraprofessionals in counseling centers. *Personnel and Guidance Journal,* 1973, *51,* 417-418.

Stollak, G. E. The experimental effects of training college students as play therapists. In Guerney, B. G., Jr. (Ed.), *Psychotherapeutic agents: New roles for nonprofessionals, parents and teachers.* New York: Holt, Rinehart & Winston, 1969.

Introduction: College Peer Counseling and Self-help Perspectives   23

APGA Sub-Committee on support personnel. Support personnel for the counselor: Their technical and non-technical roles and preparation. *Personnel and Guidance Journal*, 1967, *45*, 860-861.

Taylor, R. D. Similarity of attitudes: An assumption in the use of support personnel in the rehabilitation of the disadvantaged. Chapter 4 in Zimpfer, D. G. (Ed.), *Paraprofessionals in counseling, guidance, and personnel services*. Washington: APGA Press, 1974.

Wagenfeld, M. O., & Robin, S. S. Reality, rhetoric and the paraprofessional: A concluding note. Chapter IV in Robin, S. S., & Wagenfeld, M. O. (Eds.), *Paraprofessionals in the human services*. New York: Human Sciences Press, 1981.

Woody, R. H. Paraprofessionalism now: Reality and responsibility. Chapter in Schauble, P. G., & Resnick, J. L. (Eds.), *Paraprofessional training: Functions, methods, and issues*. Volume II. Psychological and Vocational Counseling Center Monograph Series. Psychological and Vocational Counseling Center and Division of Continuing Education, University of Florida, 1976.

Zimpfer, D. G. (Ed.). *Paraprofessionals in counseling, guidance, and personnel services*. Washington: APGA Press, 1974.

Zunker, V. G., & Brown, W. F. Comparative effectiveness of student and professional counselors. *Personnel and Guidance Journal*, 1966, *44*, 738-743.

Section I
COUNSELING AND
ADVISING STRATEGIES

Chapter 1

TELEPHONE CRISIS COUNSELING SERVICE

JOHN KALAFAT and ANDI SCHULMAN

THE Telephone Counseling Service (TCS) at Florida State University's counseling center was established in 1970 to provide help for people experiencing emotional crises. A "crisis" was defined as any temporary and disruptive state with which a person cannot readily cope. Often the person in crisis did not have, or did not know he or she had, the internal resources (knowledge, experience, strength) or external resources (family, friends, minister) to deal with a disruptive situation. Related to such crises are the needs for information and referral on issues such as daycare, health care, or locating runaways. Some callers simply needed a listener to help struggle with a painful decision, or handle oppressive feelings of loneliness and depression.

Effective crisis intervention requires several conditions that traditional helping agencies often do not provide (Lester and Brockopp, 1976; Sinnett, 1976). Most crisis situations require temporary, immediate, and readily available attention so that problems can be dealt with before they mushroom in complexity. Disruptive personal problems are particularly likely to arise at night or over weekends when most agencies are closed. Moreover, many persons who need information or help do not know where to obtain them, nor do they have the time for a complicated bureaucracy; a more flexible intervention (Morrill et al., 1980) is required. Others prefer to remain anonymous, at least until they are assured of confidentiality. To serve such persons, TCS was established as a source of help that can be reached by simply dialing

27

28   *Peer Counseling and Self-help Groups on Campus*

a telephone number at any time, twenty-four hours a day, seven days a week. Callers' anonymity and the confidentiality of their calls were guaranteed.

Three major types of service were offered to callers. First was provision of information: telephone numbers, schedules of campus and community events, details of routine procedures of university or community life (for example, how to drop a course or where to buy an automobile license tag). The second was crisis intervention counseling by trained paraprofessional volunteers. Emphasis was placed on listening with empathy, offering emotional support, and helping the caller evaluate alternative solutions to his or her immediate problem. Counseling was usually limited to a single call. Callers who seemed to need more extensive help, or who could be more appropriately served by other agencies, were encouraged to seek assistance from the appropriate sources. Thus, the third major type of service offered by TCS was referral to campus and community agencies. Referral involved determining which agencies were most appropriate for a caller and his or her particular needs, then providing information about office hours and appointment policies to facilitate the client's contact with the agency. In some cases, referral could include helping the client to deal with ambivalent feelings about seeking help from an agency.

By developing a comprehensive referral file, TCS became a central clearinghouse for information about campus and community resources. In coordinating complementary and supplementary services with other agencies, TCS developed working agreements to provide afterhours back-up and answering services to several agencies. Groups that provide emergency transportation, volunteers who work with parents concerned about drugs, and organizations serving old age-groups listed TCS as their phone number and provided TCS with a list of their on-call volunteers. TCS was also licensed as a drug counseling and referral agency by the regional drug council.

Most of the service was carried out by volunteers as in Gordon's (1976) program. Volunteers worked at the phones in eight-hour shifts; experienced volunteers trained new volunteers; and committees of volunteers publicized the service, investigated resources, and recruited staff. Most volunteers were undergraduate students, with the remainder being graduate students and volunteers from the community. A paid half-time paraprofessional served as administrative coordinator of the service, scheduling shifts and developing statistical summaries of calls. Another paraprofessional was responsible for the day-to-day updating of the resources, while a third paraprofessional acted as coordinator of the training program. A clinical psychologist on the staff of the counseling center served as overall coordinator of the service.

At any one time there were about thirty trained volunteers and thirty volunteer trainees working on the service. The number of shifts expected of each person depended upon the ratio of trained volunteers to the number of shifts in a month. The paraprofessional staff coordinators were on call at all times as back-up to the volunteers, with professional persons available for emergency consultation.

Initially, TCS served only the FSU campus, but late in the second year TCS began to extend its services to the greater Tallahassee community. This change was a relatively slow process because of the time it takes to develop relationships with community services and identify community resources. Furthermore, it seemed important to establish a solid record of service to the campus before attempting the more complex task of serving the community.

The response to the service, from both the campus and community, was favorable as reflected in the volume of calls increasing steadily from thirty to 1000 per month over a four-year period. A stratified sample of 463 students was questioned about the service after it had been in operation for seven months, and 45 percent had heard about the service despite inadequate funds for publicity. Of those familiar with the service, 82 percent stated that they thought it could provide help with personal problems, 91 percent believed it could furnish accurate information, and 90 percent trusted it to protect callers' confidentiality.

Issues Involved in the Use of Paraprofessionals

The Telephone Counseling Service began as a paraprofessional program based on a proposal developed by a team of graduate

30   *Peer Counseling and Self-help Groups on Campus*

students and supported by the director of the university counseling center. The graduate students were the original staff and the first trainers assisted by psychologists and social workers on the staff of the counseling center. These professionals worked closely with the core staff of student volunteers to organize and implement the service.

Though TCS enjoyed the input of a number of professionals, there was a concerted effort to maintain the volunteer service orientation in which professionals adopted supervisory, consultative (Morrill et al., 1980) and training (Dixon and Burns, 1975) roles. Except for one professional psychologist and three paid paraprofessional coordinators, TCS personnel were unpaid volunteers, predominately undergraduates or volunteers from the community with little or no background in the helping professions. The professional coordinator supervised and trained paraprofessional trainers and coordinators, who then supervised and trained the staff of approximately forty volunteers, who in turn handled more than 1000 calls a month. Students served as telephone counselors, participated in defining overall service goals, participated in administrative decision-making, and trained new personnel (Kalafat and Tyler, 1973).

The use of student paraprofessionals corresponds with the broad goal of higher education to support student development, such as increased sensitivity to human problems, awareness of the complexities of a community, willingness to accept responsibility, and an ability to cooperate with others.

For students who planned to enter the mental health professions, the program offered training opportunities that were not available in many training settings. Trainees in traditional placements often found that they performed specific tasks, such as counseling with a particular client or consulting with a particular elementary school teacher, but gained little insight into the overall functioning of the program or agency. Since TCS was a relatively small program which sought to involve students in all aspects of its operation, they could grasp and influence the total operation. They were involved in its administrative structure, personnel problems, and community relations. They surveyed the needs of the client population, and researched the policies on legal and ethical issues. Although the professional staff was always available for supervision or consultation, students often assumed responsibilities which ranged from teaching each other how to counsel suicidal callers to developing and implementing procedures for situations in which a mishandled call could make the volunteer liable for prosecution. Accepting such responsibilities under professional guidance provided a developmental bridge between the role of student and that of a mental health paraprofessional.

Recruiting volunteers from both student and community populations was based on the principle of employing mental health personnel from the populations being served. Such volunteers brought with them a valuable understanding both of the stresses and the supports in the community. They were often more responsive to their peers than professional counselors and often better received by them. Their training allowed them to return to their communities and their private and professional lives with enhanced sensitivity and counseling skills.

Although the emphasis on volunteer responsibility was important, it was not without problems. Students sometimes found it difficult to shed the relative safety of their traditionally passive roles. Many volunteers failed to realize that unexciting tasks like hanging posters or negotiating with the telephone company can be vital to the functioning of the program. TCS found that an individual who wanted to learn to help others does not necessarily want to become involved in fund raising. While volunteers were expected to perform many different tasks, the motivation and interests of individual volunteers were respected by recruiting a wide variety of volunteers for specific functions such as fund raising or publicity.

The commitment to volunteer staff presented problems for professional staff as well. Professional staff sought to resist the tendency to do things themselves, whether from habit, interest in the problem at hand, or fear that the volunteers will not function adequately. Nothing is more damaging to the morale and enthusiasm of a volunteer staff than to have a coordinator become the sole moving force of the service. Not only must professional staff resist interfering, but they also must resist strong pressures from outside agencies to identify a single individual as responsible

32   *Peer Counseling and Self-help Groups on Campus*

for the service. Agencies and individuals prefer to deal with the professional "in charge" rather than a volunteer.

Another and somewhat paradoxical problem arises from the recruitment of too many volunteers. Volunteers need a high level of commitment and participation. If too many of them are associated with a service, it may become difficult for an individual to see his or her role as vital or even important. Furthermore, the skills involved in providing crisis services are difficult to maintain if they must go unpracticed because the volunteer only works on a shift once every two weeks.

Finally, no matter what level of commitment and morale a service is able to maintain among its volunteers, it was important to monitor the level of burnout after a year or so. Some volunteers remained with the service longer by taking roles other than answering the phones. Positions such as resource coordinator and trainer were open only to volunteers within the service, and provided valuable experience in training, administration, and community assessment.

Former volunteers have applied their TCS skills and experience to other settings. Several were among the paraprofessional core in the development of Project Alteract, and a TCS trainer was the first paraprofessional administrative aide in the Division of Student Affairs. Still others have carried their skills into nursing, police work, VISTA, and drug abuse program management.

Selection and Training of Volunteers

A clinical psychologist and a paraprofessional coordinator directed, trained, and supervised the paraprofessionals who trained and supervised the volunteer staff. Consultants and guest speakers augmented the training program.

Schedule. Volunteers made a commitment of eight hours a week, which included two two-hour training sessions, a one-hour staff meeting, a two-hour daytime shift on the phones, and miscellaneous feedback sessions, committee meetings, and resource investigation. Though the pace was tailored to individual ability, training time averaged a total of eighty hours over a ten-week period. When the trainees were ready for supervised phone duty, usually two eight-hour shifts, they answered phones in the presence of an experienced volunteer. They were cleared for solo phone duty on the basis of feedback from the supervising volunteers according to communication skills and the command of resource information. Before being cleared for phone duty, a typical volunteer received nearly 100 hours of training, observation, and feedback from all of the trainers, in addition to on-going inservice training at staff meetings.

Format. Training included a didactic component consisting of lectures, tapes, and readings, and an experiential component of role playing, group feedback, and communication and awareness exercises. The two-hour training sessions, led by volunteer trainers, were devoted primarily to role playing and exercises. In the group setting, the volunteers role played both caller and counselor in practice calls taken from a selection of vignettes of various levels of risk as noted in Table 1-I. At the end of each session, the trainers completed a progress sheet summarizing the feedback for each trainee, which is displayed in Table 1-II. These progress sheets were kept for the trainees so that they could note their progress and areas in need of improvement.

Table 1-I

SELECTED ROLE PLAY VIGNETTES
(Male Caller)

1. (Practice). I have to live with my parents to save money and they can't get used to the idea that I'm not a little kid anymore. How can I prove it to them?
2. I just transferred here from junior college, and everybody here really seems to be into sexual relations. I'm getting real pressure from the kids I live with to have sex with my dates. Do you think this is right? (Really push and manipulate for advice)
3. (Depressed). It's terrible to grow old and not be needed anymore. I've retired and my children are all gone – they never write or call. I feel so useless – no good for anything or anybody. There's no future.
4. I really have a problem. I'm 5'2" and there aren't many girls shorter than that – and even they don't like to date short guys. I haven't had a date in months and I don't know what to do. (Nothing they suggest satisfies you)
5. I just got laid off from my job – just let go. I've been with that firm for 20 years and now I don't know if I can find another job. What am I going to do?
6. I've been having such strange thoughts and feelings lately about some of the guys on the floor. I think its been coming to this for some time now – I think I'm homosexual but I'm afraid and don't know what to do about it.
7. My girlfriend just broke up with me. I don't understand how she can say she loves me for six months and now, suddenly, she doesn't anymore. Could you please explain her to me?

34 *Peer Counseling and Self-help Groups on Campus*

Table 1-II

TELEPHONE COUNSELING SERVICE

Trainee Progress Sheet

Name:

Date:

Trainer:

Call received:

Feedback given by trainer:

Feedback given by group:

Response of trainee:

Call given: Chosen _____ Assigned _____

Terrifics:

Not-so-hots:

Suggestions for next session:

Additional comments:

    The weekly staff meetings were devoted to TCS business and in-service training for trained volunteers and trainees alike. The program consisted of lectures, exercises, and staffing particular calls or problems.

    Trainees were required to work one two-hour phone shift between 8:00 A.M. and 5:00 P.M. when most incoming calls related to information rather than personal crises. A trained volunteer was always present in the room to serve as a back-up for consultation or help in finding a certain piece of information. Trainees were instructed to transfer all counseling calls to trained volunteers. These supervised daytime shifts proved to be an excellent way to learn how to handle phone duty.

Trainers held a two-hour meeting at the beginning of each week to discuss trainees' progress and to develop and practice specific training strategies. They reviewed each trainee's progress and made specific recommendations for the coming week. For example, they might agree that the trainee should role play a particular problem or work with a certain trainer. The trainers shared materials and exercises dealing with training issues and strategies. They might, for instance, practice small group leadership skills or discuss their models of helpful behavior.

Student volunteers received up to six hours of credit at the graduate and undergraduate levels through the university Department of Psychology. Approximately 100 volunteers were trained annually.

Training goals. Because of the wide variety of problems presented to a telephone counseling service and because no single technique or counseling strategy has been demonstrated to be universally effective, the training did not emphasize specific techniques. Rather, an attempt was made to encourage each trainee to develop his or her own helping style around some broad principles.

This emphasis might lead to the following training sequence: (1) Provide trainees with an opportunity to become aware of themselves as helping persons and to begin developing a helping style. (2) Present them with general theories and trainers' concepts of helping behavior using modeling, and both didactic and experiential training components. (3) Allow them to choose from this menu of helping strategies those that fit into their developing helping styles. If they choose not to adopt some of the theory and practices presented, allow them to substitute their own and test these in training through role playing and feedback.

Training Objectives and Procedures

Though the training was designed to acquaint volunteers with all of the areas noted below, the major focus of an individual student's activity at any time was determined by his or her interests and level of experience. For example, volunteers typically devoted most of their time at first to developing their counseling skills and familiarizing themselves with community resources. As they gained experience, they became more involved in training and administration. Volunteers who were interested in research devoted most of their time to this area, while others limited their research participation to evaluating proposed or ongoing services.

1. Assessing the mental health needs of the community being served, preparing themselves to deal with problems that members of various sub-groups are likely to present.
2. Becoming familiar with community resources.
   a. Learning to assess the overall pattern of resources in the community; becoming aware of general areas of strength and weakness. Becoming alert to the importance of inter-agency cooperation; learning to work with other agencies and make referrals appropriately.
   b. Learning to investigate individual agencies in the community; discovering what information about them is necessary and ways of obtaining the information.
3. Functioning as crisis intervention counselors. Becoming aware of their impact as helping persons. Learning to assess the nature and seriousness of a presenting problem, determine the nature of the client's internal and external resources, and guide the client in seeking alternative solutions to his or her problems.
4. Becoming sensitive to relevant professional and ethical issues.
5. Carrying out training and supervision of less experienced students.
6. Administering a mental health program.
7. Evaluating the operation of a program and its effects on the community.

In the following outline of the procedures to achieve the training goals, the modules appear in the order in which they were introduced to the trainees. The order of topic presentations needs to be viewed in a flexible manner. For example, though it may make sense to provide trainees with a firm orientation to standard operating procedures and some theory before they begin role playing, it may become obvious that trainees are quickly bored with purely didactic training, and role playing might need to be introduced early in the training program.

I. **General Orientation**

This section consisted of a general history of TCS, a rationale for the service, and orientation to the TCS materials and room. The trainers, volunteers, and trainees discussed why they were in TCS and shared their goals and expectations as well as their needs or desires to be helping persons.

II. **Feedback**

Since feedback was an important part of training in addition to being useful as a helping technique, trainees were provided with specific directions for giving it and an opportunity to practice that skill. Trainers roll played calls, modeled appropriate and inappropriate feedback, and discussed the impact that the feedback had upon them. Following this, trainees divided into dyads and worked through the same process.

III. **Development of Self As a Helping Instrument**

A number of training procedures were used in an effort to help the trainees develop an awareness of themselves as helping persons.

A. It was important initially to create an atmosphere in which the trainee would feel safe to explore and to express parts of himself or herself without fear of criticism, attack, pressure to conform, or intolerance of different styles. An attempt was made to establish trust and group cohesiveness through modeling, in which the trainers engaged in self-disclosure through exercises and a variety of informal activities such as potluck dinners.

B. Trainees were supported with opportunities to see strengths in their helping behaviors through low-risk role playing and fairly simple mock calls. Through these experiences, trainees developed a foundation of helping skills and strategies on which to build. Trainees were not told that they were working with "easy calls" nor were they asked to choose calls that they felt would be easy for them. If they were to receive negative feedback under those circumstances, it might prove unnecessarily discouraging. Instead, fifty undergraduate psychology students were asked to rate each of 100 telephone vignettes as low-risk or high-risk calls for anyone to handle and the results were used to build a continuum of examples with increasing risk.

C. The trainees were videotaped in order to identify gaps in their helping styles. As part of the research program investigating the efficacy of the training program, selected trainees were required to role play each of seven difficult vignettes for ten minutes in rapid succession with no feedback. While this was a somewhat harrowing experience, it proved to be a tremendous motivating and growth experience for the trainees who went through it. They were eager to start training and begin work on their needs, as demonstrated in the role playing situation. Efforts were made to debrief trainees after the taping in order to clarify the intended purpose of the exercise.

D. A variety of awareness exercises were designed to illustrate specific issues in the helping relationship, such as the need to control or provide answers. These exercises helped the volunteers become aware of their biases, fears, needs, sore spots, and fantasies so that they could separate their concerns from those of the callers.

IV. **Presentation of Our Model of Helpful Behavior**

Throughout the didactic and experiential components of training we explicitly shared models of helpful behaviors with trainees so that they could have an opportunity to react to them openly and directly. In an effort to help trainers become aware of their concepts of helpful behavior and articulate them, trainers were asked to complete the following statements: "I am helpful when I ..., I am not helpful when I ..., A helpful person should ..., A helpful person should not ..." These statements were collected from the trainers, categorized and summarized in a training handout.

V. **Specific Helping Strategies**

The following list of helping strategies and exercises for developing skills was used in the training:

A. Listening

1. Working in dyads.

   a. Repeating what the partner says before answering him or her.

   b. Trying to talk while the partner continually interrupts.

   c. Role playing a call in which the caller includes many silences. Silences are similar to a projective stimulus. The person breaking the silence fills it, or projects into it, his or her own needs. The trainee has a choice of projecting his or her own needs or letting the caller do so.

2. Recording role playing to demonstrate listening patterns.

B. Empathy

It has become evident that being helpful involves an ability to tune into the caller's immediate feelings. This is often a difficult process in dealing with someone who looks at the world from a totally different point of view, or who is going through a problem which you have never had to consider yourself.

1. Sex reversal.

2. Exploring empathic potential.

   In certain vignettes, the caller is upset because of a value he or she holds that the trainee is unlikely to share. Take for example a caller who is very angry because he discovers that his new wife is not a virgin. Trainees often try to show this caller that there's nothing to be upset about, rather than to accept how he feels.

C. Understanding
  1. Learning to focus on the problem.
     The trainer stops the role playing and asks the trainee/counselor to state the caller's problem as he or she hears it; the trainee/caller gives feedback to check his or her accuracy.
  2. Discovering problems that a trainee typically misses. For example, a trainee often has a tendency "not to hear" one of a caller's problems if the trainee is struggling with a similar problem.
D. Action
  1. Resolving the call: What action was taken?
  2. Making referrals: Are they appropriate or buck-passing?
  3. Terminating the call: Was the caller ready?
  4. Assuming responsibility: Does the volunteer assume responsibility or allow the caller to do so?
     a. "I've got the answers"
     b. Needs to control
     c. Fallacy of the "correct solution"

VI. **Specific Call Situations**
Toward the end of training, trainees role played and discussed specific calls such as drugs, suicide, and runaways. They usually expressed a desire to practice particular calls about which they had concerns. Trainers may have had some questions about a certain volunteer's preparation for dealing with a given kind of call and wanted him or her to practice.

Program Evaluation

The initial evaluation of our program began with a student knowledge and attitude survey about the Telephone Counseling Service. In general, the results indicated that a majority of the students were aware of the service and had confidence in the ability of the service to carry out its functions. There did not appear to be any differences in awareness or attitudes about TCS by living area, class level, or sex. Majors in the natural sciences did appear to know least about TCS and were less inclined to predict that they would feel more the need to use TCS than majors in such areas as humanities, social sciences, business, and preprofessional training. The survey indicated that most students did not plan ahead to call TCS, but turned to TCS to meet a spur-of-the-moment need. This finding influenced the publicity of the TCS phone numbers by continuously and conspicuously publishing them daily in the student newspaper and broadcasting them in radio spot announcements. Wallet-size calendar cards displaying TCS phone numbers were also distributed.

While our on-campus survey required considerable effort in securing student records and classroom contact, it was more manageable than the considerable expense and logistics of conducting a survey of the greater community.

We have evaluated the impact of the TCS training program on our volunteer counselors by comparing the performance of TCS trainees to a control group in a pre- and post-training design by means of several objective personality measures. Also, many different behaviors and skills have been found to be necessary for paraprofessionals in their roles as active helpers (France, 1975). Trainees were also compared to controls on ratings of their responses while role-playing counseling vignettes of problems. These data have been analyzed with the following questions in mind: Do initial differences exist between trainees and controls? What relationships exist among measures? Can we predict performance in role playing from any of the scales or from written responses to vignettes? Can we predict performance and progress in training, as indicated by trainers' feedback, from any of the measures? Tyler et al., (1978) report the results of rating responses to vignettes along the dimensions of affectiveness, understanding, and problem exploration. Kalafat et al., (1979) report results of analyzing untrained, newly trained, and experienced and trained paraprofessionals in terms of therapeutic responses to counseling calls reflected in written scripts. This study separates the experience and training variables, supports the positive role of training, and notes a complex relationship between values and performance that needs further study. Other kinds of comparative studies such as that by O'Donnell and George (1977) are also needed to broaden our understanding of paraprofessionalism.

Conclusion

The Telephone Counseling Service began as a program to provide a nontraditional approach to meet the specific, time-limited needs of university students. It evolved into a major provider of crisis and referral service to the greater community and became an important component of the human service delivery system. The program to train paraprofessional volunteers has grown to include a number of training strategies and variety of training issues for students interested in the helping professions. TCS has expanded its role in the community as a twenty-four-hour crisis center and as a central clearinghouse for information and referrals for a local community mental health center and drug abuse agency.

REFERENCES

Dixon, M. C., & Burns, J. L. The training of telephone crisis intervention volunteers. *American Journal of Community Psychology*, 1975, *3*, 145-150.

France, K. Evaluation of lay volunteer crisis telephone workers. *American Journal of Community Psychology*, 1975, *3*, 197-200.

Gordon, J. S. Youth helping youth. *Social Policy*, 1976, *7*(2), 48-53.

Kalafat, J. D., Boroto, D. R., & France, K. Relationships among experience level and value orientation and the performance of paraprofessional telephone counselors. *American Journal of Community Psychology*, 1979, *7*(2), 167-180.

Kalafat, J. D., & Tyler, M. The community approach: Programs and implications for a campus mental health agency. *Professional Psychology*, 1973, *4*(1), 43-59.

Lester, D., & Brockopp, G. W. (Eds.). *Crisis intervention and counseling by telephone*. Springfield, Ill.: Charles C Thomas, Publisher, 1976.

Morrill, W. H., Oetting, E. R., & Hurst, J. C. The method of intervention. Chapter 8 in Morrill, W. H., & Hurst, J. C. (Eds.), *Dimensions of intervention for student development*. New York: John Wiley & Sons, 1980.

O'Donnell, J. M., & George, K. The use of volunteers in a community mental health center emergency and reception service: A comparative study of professional and lay telephone counseling. *Community Mental Health Journal*, 1977, *13*, 3-12.

Sinnett, E. R. *Crisis services for campus and community: A handbook for the volunteer*. Springfield, Ill.: Charles C Thomas, Publisher, 1976.

Tyler, M., Kalafat, J. D., Boroto, D. R. & Hartman, J. A brief assessment technique for paraprofessional helpers. *Journal of Community Psychology*, 1978, *6*, 53-59.

Chapter 2

CURRICULAR-CAREER INFORMATION SERVICE

ROBERT REARDON, CAROLE S. MINOR, and MARY BURKHART

THE Curricular-Career Information Service (CCIS) was developed as an outreach, self-help, multimedia-based, career guidance program for students at Florida State University. It utilized a variety of resources — human, institutional, and material — which include career information in printed (Holland, 1970) and audiovisual forms, instructional modules, referral resources, and student "resident assistants" (RA's) placed in undergraduate living units. Career guidance and academic advisement programs at Florida State University have operated historically with very little coordination. In order to satisfy a range of sometimes conflicting goals, emanating from students, counselors, academic advisors, administrators, and parents, the CCIS was developed using a systems approach similar to Hosford and Ryan (1970) and Boggs (1980). This chapter describes the early development and evaluation of CCIS, which became fully operational in the mid-1970s, especially the role and training of the paraprofessionals recommended by Hoyt (1970), Hopke (1976), and Gartner et al., (1977).

Identifying Problems and Specifying Goals

Several early surveys had revealed widespread dissatisfaction with the existing advisement and career guidance program. Surveys of entering students had shown that as many as 60 percent wanted help with career information, while the service ranked second was study skills at only 10 percent (*Characteristics of College Students,* 1972; *Self-Study Report,* 1972). A Harris Poll (1970) conducted at Florida State University found 56 percent of the undergraduates somewhat to very satisfied with advising, but 44 percent dissatisfied. Fifty percent of the students were satisfied with the help they had received in choosing a major, but only 36 percent were satisfied with similar assistance in long-range career planning.

It appeared that the greatest problems were in the lower division and that there was variability in the quality of services in different schools or colleges. Services at the community colleges that feed into the university were perceived to be as limited as in the senior institution. The smaller schools and colleges appeared to provide better services than the larger units in the university. Students were found to rely more on their peers and on their personal resourcefulness in career and academic planning than on faculty or other university services (Pierce, 1970), an especially important point because a student-to-student approach might be particularly appropriate for advising and career services as Gartner et al., (1977) and Panther (1976) have suggested. Indeed, the Harris Poll (1970) also showed that many faculty members were not interested in providing academic advisement and related services to students. Generally they were poorly equipped in terms of necessary resources, inadequately trained to do the job, and there was little incentive for them to improve since advisement counted little toward promotion and tenure.

The lack of university-wide coordination was also a problem (Winner, 1973). Orientation, admissions, junior college articulation, placement, and vocational counseling were largely provided through the Division of Student Affairs or other special offices, whereas advisement was under the Division of Academic Affairs. The academic advisement and career guidance needs of students were thus splintered in the administrative gap between student and academic affairs. This problem was partially remedied by a university reorganization in the mid-1970s, which placed all of the programs and services named above under the Vice-President for Student Educational Services.

Every assessment of student needs revealed an overwhelming desire for more curricular and career information. This was especially true of students who were new in the institution, those unsure about their academic or career plans, those who were in the process of making vocational decisions, and those who needed access to university information, including referral resources and trained people who could assist them in their personal development. Disgruntled students, bitter about poor advisement or career guidance services, were complaining to parents and political leaders. Improved dissemination of academic and career information to secondary schools and community colleges was also needed.

In summary, the real-life environment exhibited a number of problems in the area of academic advisement and career guidance. The complexity of the situation suggested the need for equally complex solutions. The changing job market for college graduates and the need to demonstrate public accountability forced the University to commit itself to making some changes.

After these needs were identified and available resources and interested people mobilized, it was possible to develop the following goals for improving the quality of the academic advisement and career guidance:

1. Complete the documentation of problems in career planning among college students.
2. Use a career decision-making model in developing programs to facilitate individual career planning.
3. Assist students in identifying their primary areas of academic and career interest early in their college years.
4. Help students locate and use information relevant to their most important academic and career alternatives.
5. Identify university and community resources available for assistance in the development of academic/career plans.
6. Improve coordination of the flow of academic (and career) information so that it is readily available to those who need it.
7. Use students and other paraprofessionals in the most advantageous way to promote student career development.

46 *Peer Counseling and Self-help Groups on Campus*

8. Develop resources and materials which will support the efforts of faculty advisors, counselors, and related persons.
9. Assess the improved public relations which should result from new program efforts in this area.
10. Evaluate the advantages and disadvantages of a variety of program alternatives.

CCIS Prototype

In order to reach these goals, the Curricular-Career Information Service, a multimedia based career guidance program, was developed by utilizing an extensive library of books, pamphlets, and audiovisual materials. It included about 120 audio and twenty video cassette tapes devoted to information about college majors, post-baccalaureate occupational alternatives, and relevant career development information. CCIS also included five instructional modules designed to meet the general program goals. Each module provided several alternative instructional activities and the user selected among them in meeting the objectives of the module.

After considerable experimentation, the major elements of the information service were several fifteen-minute slide-tape presentations describing CCIS, the process of career decision-making, how to locate information, selected readings on career development, Holland's *Self-Directed Search* (1970), videotapes of simulated interviews in which students and faculty members discuss academic programs in the University, and information about sources of specialized assistance for student career development.

The core CCIS staff included a half-time project director, a full-time career guidance specialist, two half-time graduate assistants working to acquire information materials and develop visuals for the slide tapes, a doctoral student with responsibilities for evaluating the program, a residence hall counselor, eight residence hall assistants, and a half-time secretary.

CCIS was first located in a three-room suite just off the main entrance in a freshmen residence hall. The area included a reading lounge, a storage area, and an equipment room. There were two multi-media equipped Howe rear screen listening-viewing carrels, one of which also had a video-cassett replay system. CCIS was expanded into new locations in the University Student Union and the College of Education.

The development and operation of prototype CCIS unit was supported by the Division of Student Affairs. The total budget for the pilot year was approximately $20,000, which did not include released time for the project director or the residence hall staff.

The acquisition and development of materials were the principal staff activities in the first six months. Initially, CCIS was in operation primarily for the 390 freshmen men and women students living in the freshmen residence hall. The unit was next opened to referrals from other residence halls, the counseling center, the placement office, and several other student services offices, and finally to any student. It has remained open twenty-five hours per week for all students in the university.

Paraprofessional Training

A key factor in the successful operation of CCIS has involved the role of the proctor or helper. Earlier it was noted that many students sought advising and career planning information from other students. It then served a natural, logical stop for the available upper division students and residence hall assistants to become the paraprofessionals used to proctor and assist with the program.

The primary group of CCIS paraprofessionals, the RAs, first went through a training program that was designed to help them in dealing with people. They next went through training specific to CCIS. Because their earlier RA training was relevant to their ability to assist students in CCIS, it is described briefly below.

The university required that resident assistants (RAs) have a minimum grade point average of 2.0 or above and sophomore standing. RAs were typically selected from a pool of applicants several times larger than the number of vacancies. Some students were encouraged to apply by a residence counselor or a current RA. RAs were selected by a process in which they were put into simulated situations in the areas of administration, programming, and human relations-crisis intervention that they might encounter as an RA. Staff members then evaluated them on their performances.

48   *Peer Counseling and Self-help Groups on Campus*

RAs received two kinds of training. The first consisted of a retreat during which the RAs were instructed in university and residence hall procedures, engaged in two or more sessions of human relations training, and took part in several formal discussions of issues surrounding the campus and student life. The second phase of training was tailored to the unique situation presented by each residence hall. This included group leadership training, human relations exercises, and familiarization with the procedures and regulations relating to their particular residence hall. It was at this stage that the RAs were introduced to the workings of CCIS and their role in its operations.

CCIS Training

Resident assistants and other paraprofessionals in CCIS, including interns in counseling, higher education, and career development, went through a training program that oriented them to the information available in CCIS and how to use it, as well as to methods for dealing with problems that students might experience. The CCIS training program consisted of eight, one and one-half hour training sessions; twelve to sixteen hours of outside work; and three three-hour on-the-job experiences with the CCIS under supervision.

Session one included an introduction to the program and its purpose and development; a discussion of the role of the helper in CCIS; and instructions on operating procedures, equipment operation, and making referrals. Trainees were requested to go through all instructional modules and attempt to familiarize themselves with the program before the next session. This took about four hours. The second session was devoted to a review of materials available and a critique of the instructional modules and slidetape presentations. Trainees were given a list of questions designed to familiarize them with the materials and requested to complete them before the fifth session. In the third session, the use of the *Dictionary of Occupational Titles* and other standard references was explained. Sessions four and five consisted of a review of the assigned questions. The last three sessions were devoted to role playing situations based on actual situations occurring in CCIS.

After trainees completed all the training sessions, they were assigned duty for three afternoons with someone who had experience working in CCIS. Inservice training of CCIS proctors included periodic information sessions about new materials or services available, critiques of program materials, sessions to discuss operational problems, and discussions of unique situations that occur and ways of handling them. Cooperation between paraprofessionals and professional staff was required at each stage of training and supervision, just as Peterson et al., (1970) have found elsewhere.

Operating Procedures

The twenty-five hours per week was varied so as to include afternoons, evening hours, and some weekend time. Interns and the Career Development Specialist proctored CCIS during the afternoons; the RAs staffed CCIS during the evening hours and on weekends. Typically, the work involved the tasks below.

1. Greeting a student as he or she entered.
2. Explaining the purposes of CCIS, what was available and how it was to be used.
3. Helping the student select an appropriate module or other material with which to begin the program.
4. Demonstrating use of the audiovisual equipment.
5. Explaining the filing system, if necessary.
6. Helping the student select additional appropriate activities.
7. Referring a student who needed additional help to an appropriate service such as the University Counseling Center.
8. Encouraging students to fill out evaluation forms.

There were various ways for students to use CCIS materials. Some who entered expressed curiosity about the purpose and function of the unit, or expressed general concern with the choice of a major. Others expressed specific needs to learn about themselves or about particular major fields of study or occupational areas.

From the options available to the students, they tended to use the modules in the following sets: (1) the introductory module and those on career decision-making guidelines and information sources made one such set, (2) the introductory module and the self-assessment module, and (3) bypassing the modules and making direct use of the materials file or the CCIS library. All students were encouraged to evaluate CCIS modules and materials.

The effective operation of CCIS required constant cooperation between residence hall personnel and other units within the university. Residence hall counselors directly related to CCIS helped to publicize CCIS to residents as well as supervise RAs. Resident counselors and RAs from other residence halls were invited to visit CCIS and become familiar with what it could offer to their students.

Referrals to CCIS were solicited from the Counseling Center, the Placement Office, academic advisors and other units on campus. Publicity on campus included presentations to various student organizations, radio announcements, newspaper articles, posters in prominent areas and a wide distribution of brochures. An important liaison was developed with the orientation office and CCIS staff members participated in many orientation activities similar to those advocated by Conroy (1978).

Evaluating the Program

Both formative and summative evaluations had been made of the CCIS even before it became fully operational (Smith, 1973). The effectiveness of the five modules and of all materials used in CCIS were analyzed. User reactions were obtained from printed forms or stenotaped dictations to determine whether or not CCIS activities enabled students to meet the program goals stated earlier. The differential use of CCIS among the students living in the residence hall was analyzed by sex, fields of study, and so forth. Observations from the RAs, reactions from about 100 visitors, and comments from faculty advisors were also included in the evaluation.

A comparison group of students in another coed freshmen residence hall was also studied to aid in determining the effectiveness of CCIS. These students did not have access to CCIS, but were able to use all of the existing university resources for career planning assistance. A posttest-only design allowed for comparison of the two groups on such criterion measures as career maturity (Crites, 1973), knowledge and use of university resources in career development, satisfaction with current academic/career plans, and level of career decision-making (Harren, 1972). A questionnaire constructed especially for this part of the evaluation was used in conjunction with two published instruments (Smith, 1973).

At the end of the pilot phase, about half of the residents in the experimental group completed a questionnaire regarding CCIS, and 45 percent reported using the service. Most students used at least two types of media and 77 percent spent from a few minutes to two hours in CCIS. Seventy percent agreed or strongly agreed that the materials were helpful to them, while 23 percent were neutral and eight percent disagreed. Almost 80 percent of the students agreed that the CCIS materials lent themselves to self-directed use. Finally, both users and nonusers agreed that academic advisement material should be included in CCIS (84 percent), and that CCIS should be recommended to a freshman needing career development assistance (91 percent).

Experience with the CCIS program to date indicated that the selection, training and supervision of the paraprofessional helper was a critical variable in the success of the program. The residence hall location and the proctoring of the RAs has been a positive feature; that the RAs knew the program well has facilitated student use of CCIS. However, on the negative side, the performance of the RAs was sometimes questionable due to their lack of skills, disinterest, and lack of supervision. Improvements in the design of CCIS were made in order to simplify the technical aspect of the program so that minimally trained paraprofessionals can proctor it more effectively.

In the outcome phase of the pilot evaluation, no differences were found on the *CMI Attitude Scale* or *VOC* for the experimental group users, the experimental group nonusers, or the comparison group. However, a Dunn *Multiple Comparisons Procedure* showed CCIS users were better able to identify and use university resources for their personal career development than the nonusers (.05) or the comparison groups (.01). CCIS users also indicated they had learned more about the career decision-making process in the five months of the pilot program than the CCIS nonusers (.01) or the comparison group (.01).

Implications

Due to the success of CCIS in meeting many of its objectives in the pilot phase, the program was continued, modified and expanded. It was apparent that the successful operation of a CCIS-type program and the use of paraprofessionals were dependent on meeting the following conditions:

1. The program must be largely self-help in nature, so that part-time paraprofessionals will not have to master a technical, complex procedure for locating information or routing people through the program.
2. The paraprofessionals must be warm and supportive in their initial contacts with students wanting help. They must greet people quickly upon entering, and generally convey support and helpfulness through their actions.
3. The administrative and office support services required for a CCIS-type program were considerable. This included clerical assistance, professional staff back-up services, appropriate office space, and salaries.
4. As with most other outreach programs, unit location, continuous evaluation, publicity, and personnel selection were key variables in the successful operation of a CCIS-type program.

REFERENCES

Board of Regents Staff. *Characteristics of college students—undergraduate.* Tallahassee: State University System of Florida, 1972.

Boggs, K. R. Career decision making. Chapter 18 in Morrill, W. H., & Hurst, J. C. (Eds.). *Dimensions of intervention for student development.* New York: John Wiley & Sons, 1980.

Conroy, J. K. Paid student paraprofessionals. *National Association of Student Personnel Administration Journal,* 1978, *15,* 18-24.

Crites, J. *Career maturity inventory.* Monterey: California Test Bureau/ McGraw-Hill, 1973.

Gartner, A., Riessman, F., & Jackson, V. C. (Eds.). *Paraprofessionals today. Volume I: Education.* New York: Human Sciences Press, 1977.

Harren, V. Vocational decision making checklist. Mimeographed. Carbondale: Southern Illinois University, 1972. (Available from the author.)

Harris, L., & Associates. Study prepared for Florida State University. Poll conducted at Florida State University, Tallahassee, April 1972. Mimeographed.

Holland, J. *The self-directed search: A guide to educational and vocational planning.* Palo Alto: Consulting Psychologists Press, 1970.

Hopke, W. E. Vocational paraprofessional or support personnel as a part of guidance team. *Vocational Guidance Quarterly,* 1976, *25*(2), 130-137.

Hosford, R., & Ryan, T. A. Systems design in the development of counseling and guidance programs. *Personnel and Guidance Journal,* 1970, *49,* 221-230.

Hoyt, K. B. Vocational guidance for all: New kinds of personnel needed. *American Vocational Journal,* 1970, *45*(5), 62-65.

Johnson, C., director. University self-study report. Mimeographed. Tallahassee: Florida State University, 1972.

Panther, E. F. Career education's missing link: Support personnel. *Florida Vocational Journal,* 1976, *1*(4), 13-15.

Peterson, E. F., Rowe, F. A., & Whiting, L. R. Professional-paraprofessional cooperation in career development. *Personnel and Guidance Journal,* 1974, *52,* 412-417.

Pierce, D. An investigation of problems perceived in conjunction with junior college students transferring to a senior institution. Unpublished Ph.D. dissertation, Florida State University, 1970.

Smith, J. D. The evaluation of a multimedia based self-directed career development program for college freshmen. Unpublished Ph.D. dissertation, Florida State University, 1973.

Winner, J. A systems analysis of the academic advisement/career development program at Florida State University. Mimeographed. Tallahassee: Florida State University, 1973.

Chapter 3

A CAMPUS DRUG INFORMATION
AND SERVICE CENTER

ALEXANDER BASSIN

FOR nearly two decades the extent and management of the drug abuse problem has been a pervasive concern of university administrators. Local news media, campus newspapers, university administrators and faculty, local police, parents, and social service agencies all worry about the students' use of marijuana, amphetamines, uppers, downers, LSD, ludes, cocaine, and heroin. The university organizes faculty conferences to cope with the problem; and ad hoc committees are formed that issue reports, manifestos, and action plans. Nearly everyone appears to be concerned about drug abuse except the student who comes to class "zonked out of his or her mind," with eyes barely open, staring vacantly at the blackboard like an overdosed mental patient. Many drug users, marijuana users in particular, tend to feel they are in perfect control and have no need for counseling or any other university service relating to drug education.

The client for a drug-counseling program differs from the typical patient receiving psychotherapy in almost every essential way. He or she is not motivated for the treatment and usually does not want it. In addition, many of our counseling procedures are geared to a client who is in such pain that he or she will make sacrifices to obtain therapy. As Glasser (1972) notes, the middle class neurotic who suffers the deep pain of loneliness and alienation seeks relief by talking to and become involved in a relationship with a trained professional. In contrast, the drug user has already discovered a medicine to ease his or her excruciating pangs of loneliness by taking a pill, smoking pot, taking a cube of LSD, snorting some coke, or injecting some heroin. Thus, students become their own doctor, complete with prescriptions, and would like to be left alone.

With these problems in mind, the administration and faculty on the Florida State University campus decided, after much discussion, to seek funding from the Law Enforcement Assistance Administration for a community drug information and service center (DISC).

The DISC House (an acronym for Drug Information and Service Center) established solid lines of communication with campus security, city police, and the sheriff's office as well as with the disciplinary arm of the university administration. The community was notified of the existence of this resource by newspaper, radio and television. All service agencies and both high school and elementary school guidance counselors were told of this new facility for coping with the drug abuse problem.

The DISC House program offered a responsible alternative to wrecking a kid's life by arrest, conviction and commitment to an institution through intense paraprofessional counseling (Reinstein, 1973; Rudow, 1974; Scott, 1981) and close supervision under the direction of experienced and qualified staff. Referrals were received from police, sheriff's officers, social workers and teachers among others.

The Program of Reality Therapy

The underlying philosophy and the mode of treatment employed at DISC House was based on the work of Glasser (1965, 1968, 1972). The basic premise is that those who fool with drugs need to develop a drug substitute based on constructive involvement with people to overcome feelings of loneliness, alienation and low self-worth by engaging in responsible behavior to win self-esteem.

The staff at DISC House was trained to be warm, friendly, and accepting of the new client. They slowly and patiently oriented participants to the basic rules of the house, no violence of any kind and no chemicals or alcohol.

The DISC House staff radiated concern and acceptance. The paraprofessional staff composed of experienced students was highly personal in terms of relating their own backgrounds (Trader, 1975; Siassi et al., 1977) of drug abuse (if it happened to have been part of their own experience) and the "rocky road" to recovery and improved self-concept. Staff listened patiently to complaints and self-pitying comments from the new client in order to keep the client from quitting the program. Otherwise, the staff might be viewed as unfeeling, unsympathetic, or uninformed about dope. In addition to listening to the client's repeated complaints about feeling depressed and reports of psychosomatic ailments, efforts are made to understand specific behaviors, using Glasser's Reality Therapy approach of eliciting the minutiae of daily existence. Through active, nonjudgmental listening, the counselor seeks information about eating, sleeping, and leisure habits as reflected in the following dialogue:

Paraprofessional Counselor: I dig that you are depressed but tell me what you are doing.

Stan: What do you mean what am I doing? I'm feeling miserable.

Paraprofessional Counselor: Yes, yes, I know that. But what are you doing? How are you spending the time of the day when you're not here at the House?

Stan: You really want to know that crap?

Professional Counselor: Exactly. Give me a blow-by-blow, hour-by-hour story of what you do. For example, what did you do yesterday? Start from the beginning. When did you get up?

Stan: I stay at home, watch television, eat and sometimes go around the block for a walk. My probation officer told me to stay away from my old friends and out of bars and pool halls. It's really a drag.

Paraprofessional Counselor: What do you think of the kind of life you lead? Is it doing you any good? Is it helping you reach your goals in life?

These last few questions are the most critical aspects of the Reality Therapy process. In seeking to build a relationship, the counselor comes across as a warm, friendly person who is prepared to discuss any problem of mutual interest by reflecting his own life experiences in the context of accepting, nonjudgmental conversation. The counselor needs to be an interesting, optimistic, and nice person to have as a friend and companion.

A Campus Drug Information and Service Center   57

By encouraging Stan to talk about his life goals and his values, the counselor poses questions in a mood of resolving a value of mutual interest. Is your behavior helping you reach the goals you want? He waits for the client to work through his rationalizations and worries about failure. If the client insists that he is satisfied with his life and has no intention of changing, the counselor does not argue. He merely suggests that the client think over the matter, and they turn to other topics for discussion. In a few days, the counselor may again make an opportunity for the client to make a value judgment about his behavior.

As a rule, if there is even a minimal degree of involvement (friendship), the client will respond sooner or later with a negative evaluation of his behavior. At this point the counselor might begin the Reality Therapy process by brainstorming a strategy to improve Stan's daily activity and by making a plan as reflected in the following exchange:

Paraprofessional Counselor: You're not saying that your behavior has no value just to make me happy?

Stan: Hell no! You don't have to be an Einstein to see that it's getting me nowhere.

Paraprofessional Counselor: Do you have any idea, any plans, any suggestions to improve your life-style?

Stan and his friendly counselor now brainstorm a strategy to improve Stan's daily activity. He may express boredom with being at home and visiting the House. The counselor will wait until the idea emerges from Stan, but is prepared to give a gentle prompt: "Have you thought, perhaps, of returning to school?"

Stan: Hey, that would be neat. But the dean said it was out of the question. I must stay out for at least a year.

Paraprofessional Counselor: I know, but sometimes they will make an exception if they are convinced you are sincere. Are you?

Stan: What do you mean?

Paraprofessional Counselor: Do you really want to go to school?

The counselor explains that they must arrive at a mutually agreeable understanding that Stan will stick to the plan by going to all scheduled classes, doing a small amount of homework, staying away from the drug crowd. If the client insists he is serious, the counselor might gently suggest that he put his commitment to a plan into a written contract. A good plan must include small steps designed to shape gradually the ultimate behavior. It must include numerous opportunities for success, since a grandiose plan may be too overwhelming and thereby increase one's sense of failure.

At subsequent sessions, the counselor monitors the contract by discussing Stan's experiences in school. As a start, Stan registers for only two hours of classes and spends the rest of the time at the House. He is liberally reinforced with praise and expressions of hope and encouragement. If Stan falters, the counselor does not scold or threaten him with punishment, but asks if he is still committed to the contract or if he wishes to revise it. Almost every time Stan visits the House he participates in a group encounter. Here the force and creativity of his peers are mobilized to help him since they are all in the same boat and need each other's assistance.

With the passage of time Stan begins to respond to the counselor's involvement and to his close association with the other young people in the program. He is given increasing recognition and responsibility. He is asked to assist the work of the counselor by orienting newcomers. As his period of treatment progresses, Stan begins to assume more and more responsibility for counseling with fellow members of the program and to act as a role model in his relations with them. In six months to a year he has incorporated enough of the value system of the community to be able to function with only occasional "booster shots" of enthusiasm and support.

As the day of termination approaches, Stan's counselor advises him that the counselor's personal resources and those of the House are at his disposal. He is encouraged to engage in what Alcoholics Anonymous calls "Step 12 Work" by offering to act as a big brother to some young newcomer in the program and to maintain follow-up visits (Sloan and Lipscomb, 1975) to the House in order to share his story with newcomers.

DISC Village

But Glasser (1972, p. 193) tells us:

Stan may decide to enter a place such as Synanon where he can have the day-to-day support of others who have also decided to start life again without drugs. He needs successful involvement with others to increase the strengthening of his identity, which had begun at home. Synanon, Daytop Village, or Phoenix House will probably help Stan more than any individual can, since such places provide a program tailored to the drug user's intense need for personal involvement. They also provide him with opportunities to work first in, and then outside, the house. Such institutions are available in many large cities and some smaller towns. His plan to be guided . . . to one of them, it would be a big step forward.

Early in its development, it became apparent to the staff of DISC House that a facility open from 10:00 A.M. to 5:00 P.M. was simply not enough to alter the self-image and destructive behavior of very disturbed drug abusers. A residential therapeutic community was needed similar to Daytop Village (Bassin, 1970), which incorporated Glasser's principles for treating drug abuse. With the financial assistance of the State Drug Abuse Office, a proposal was drafted calling for a minimally staffed facility to house twenty-five drug abusers of varying ages. DISC Village was established in a ten-room house in the center of town after overcoming some community hostility based on the usual fears about a colony of "dope fiends" being established in their midst.

The DISC Village program was modeled after Daytop Village for hard core heroin addicts (Bassin, 1964, 1965, 1968, 1970). Special orientation rituals are used there to help assure participant involvement, such as, "You need us, we don't need you," several telephone calls are required for an appointment, and sitting in a "prospect" chair for hours before the first interview. The prospect is submitted to a harsh interview in the course of which he or she is told in street language that as an addict he or she has become an expert con-artist who knows how to manipulate counselors, social workers, and probation officers, that he or she has been sponging off his or her family shamelessly, and that Daytop is managed almost exclusively by ex-addicts who are graduates of the program and will not accept his or her con games.

At DISC Village, however, the participants were not hard core dope addicts and, therefore, a more friendly, nonabrasive involvement procedure was employed during the intake interviews. The residents were assured that DISC Village was their home and told that consideration for each other's welfare was a central feature of the program. Participants were responsible for the upkeep of the entire facility, meals were cooked by residents in rotation, and all household chores were part of the DISC Village experience. Every day began with a morning meeting designed to give residents an opportunity to speak up in democratic fashion about the operation of the facility. During the day most of the residents attended local high schools or the university. Several times a week there were group encounter sessions involving all the residents.

The DISC Village program stressed self-control. Even in groups, residents had to wait their turn, keep their seat, and refrain from making any threats of violence or harm to others. In contrast to the manner in which residents would use dope whenever anxious or experiencing interpersonal problems, the self-control method in DISC Village was called "hold and dump," in which angry feelings were held until they could be dumped in a group encounter. In addition to talking about good and bad feelings, residents were expected to confront other residents with their opinions about them. Furthermore, residents who had accumulated guilt feelings about something they had done were encouraged to spill them out in front of their "brothers and sisters" in the group.

Residents learned that holding onto resentful feelings increased their likelihood of reacting impulsively, and exploding. The more they held, the more likely it was that the next strain would push them over the edge, causing some disastrous reaction and possibly leaving the program. Drug users tend to be unusually touchy and sensitive. It is easy for them to become enraged or get their feelings hurt. They are usually unable to handle their feelings when aroused; therefore it was taboo to "react" in any situation except in a group encounter or in a private conference with a staff member. This resulted in extraordinarily loud and exciting group exchanges. In the course of a meeting, a resident's use of vulgarity and obscenity, his/her careless personal habits or his/her tendency to boast of his/her street exploits were all presented for review and examination. It was understood, however, that this material was to be exposed only for purposes of helping the resident grow and become a mature and responsible human being. Since it is common for drug abusers to experience difficulty in achieving solid interpersonal relations, program staff continuously urge residents to mingle and get to know their brothers and sisters.

DISC Village attempted to complete its treatment program for individual residents in a period of less than a year. The following case of Lois Glenn gives a firsthand view of how the program operated.

Case Study

In less than two years my life has taken a 180-degree turn. From my early teen years I had been involved in drugs in a constant progression from smoking marijuana to sticking needles in my arm. By the time I reached eighteen, I had been living away from home for over a year, and had been expelled from a major university for disciplinary reasons. When I arrived in Tallahassee, I wanted to be with the most negative type of people, and I immediately began seeking them out. At this point in my life my apparent motivation was towards drugs and my life-style was totally irresponsible. I would not work steadily, and I would not return to school because I had been expelled from another university. Any income I managed to acquire went towards the purchase of drugs, and as a result, I had turned towards various illegal activities to support myself. I stole to eat and pay my bills.

My first arrest was for the misdemeanor charge of "interfering with an officer in the line of duty," which took place when several of my friends were arrested on drug charges. After spending twenty-four hours in the county jail and submitting to a presentence investigation that lasted over two months, I was placed on two years' probation and given a strict warning by the judge. Unfortunately this incident did not serve as a strong enough warning to mend my ways. Instead, I continued consuming more and more drugs. I was blind to what I was doing to myself.

However, the motivation to do something for myself came as a result of my second arrest for the more serious charges of two felonies and a misdemeanor relating to drugs. Furthermore, since I was still on probation for my first offense, my situation was obviously extremely serious. It happens that I was busted in a motel where I had met several other drug users. I spent two weeks in the county jail and was released only after receiving warnings from my probation officer and lawyer that I could expect a prison sentence unless I became involved in some type of rehabilitation program.

My first involvement in a drug program of any type was with DISC House, a daycare facility on the Florida State University campus. Even though I was in severe legal difficulties and had a good chance of going to prison, I was still not motivated enough to make a permanent change. I was concerned only with getting out of my immediate trouble. I still looked on drugs as the only thing I wanted to do with my life.

This attitude continued for several months, even after I switched my involvement from the daycare DISC House to the more intense therapeutic environment at DISC Village, a residential program that I entered upon the instruction of my probation officer. I lived as a resident at DISC Village for almost six months and went through only minor behavioral changes while pretending to change more. My only motivation was still towards drugs, but I knew that with my legal difficulties I had to finish the program. Somehow, though, I finally came to realize that doing drugs was not as great as I had always told myself, and that I had been lying to myself about the kind of life I had been leading. When I looked honestly at how I had been living, stealing, lying, hurting people who cared about me, I finally realized that I wanted to do something better with myself. I began to work harder at changing those things about myself that had contributed to my negative life-style, my dishonesty, my lack of self-respect, my low self-confidence. I could have accomplished none of this without the DISC Village program and its staff. I was obliged to take an honest look at the kind of life I had been living.

I am now a staff member at DISC Village, trying to give some others the same help I was provided. I returned to school at Florida State University and during my last quarter in attendance I even made the Dean's List, something I would have thought impossible only two years ago. I have my own apartment and car, and I can now afford some of the things for myself that I never could before because all my money went into dope. My relationship with my family is excellent and I even get along very well with my probation officer.

It's been over a year since I've done any drugs and several months since I've moved out of the program. These last months have been the best, most productive, of my life. I still have problems, like any human being, and I still make mistakes, but I am able to deal with these problems and accept these mistakes — because I am happy with who I am.

Conclusion

At every morning meeting there was an individual or group recitation of a poem written in the early 1960s by a resident of Daytop Village at Staten Island, New York:

We are here because there is no refuge, finally, from ourselves.
Until a man confronts himself in the eyes and hearts
    Of his fellows
    He is running
Until he suffers them to share his secrets
    He has no safety from it.
Afraid to be known, he can know neither himself nor any other.
    He will be alone.

Where else but in our common ground can we find such a mirror?
Here, together, a man can at last appear clearly to himself.
    Not as the giant of his dreams
    Or the dwarf of his fears
        But as a man, part of the whole, with his share in its purposes.
In this ground we can each take root — and grow
    Not alone, anymore, as in death
    But alive, a man among men.

Though residents detected the unfortunate sexist note in the declaration, the essential meaning comes through loud and clear: we need one another to achieve even a modest measure of self-fulfillment. The DISC projects were geared to provide love, involvement, and to nurture a higher self-esteem based on responsible behavior for our own benefit and that of all of mankind. The DISC programs reflected a peer counseling approach to treatment that could be applied in a variety of settings. The key ingredient was creating an environment through which people who had spent their energies hiding from themselves could be drawn into the mainstream of human existence.

REFERENCES

Bassin, A. Daytop village — stopover or cure. *Psychology Today,* 1968, December, 48-52.

Bassin, A. Daytop village — therapeutic community for drug addicts. *Addictions,* 1970, *17,* 30-44.

Bassin, A., & Shelly, J. A. Daytop lodge: Halfway house for drug addicts. *Federal Probation,* 1964, *28,* 46-54.

Bassin, A., & Shelly, J. A. Daytop lodge: A new treatment approach for drug addicts. *Correctional Psychiatry,* 1965, *11,* 186-195.

Glasser, W. *Reality therapy: A new approach to psychiatry.* New York: Harper & Row, 1965.

Glasser, W. *Schools without failure.* New York: Harper & Row, 1968.

Glasser, W. *The identity society.* New York: Harper & Row, 1972.

Reinstein, M. J. The role of drug counselors in a hospital drug-cure program. *Hospital and Community Psychiatry,* 1973, *24*(12), 839-841.

Rudow, E. H. Paraprofessionals in a drug education program. *Personnel and Guidance Journal,* 1974, *53*(4), 294-297.

Scott, J. E. Paraprofessionals in criminal justice. Section II in Robin, S.S., & Wagenfeld, M. O. (Eds.), *Paraprofessionals in the human services.* New York: Human Sciences Press, 1981.

Siassi, I., Angle, B. P., & Alston, D. C. Who should be counselors in methadone maintenance programs: Ex-addicts or nonaddicts? *Community Mental Health Journal,* 1977, *13,* 125-132.

Sloan, J. L., & Lipscomb, W. R. A. A nonobtrusive interview technique for drug abuse program follow-up. *Community Mental Health Journal,* 1975, *11,* 368-370.

Trader, H. The ex-addict in the role of counselor. *Journal of Drug Issues,* 1975, *5,* 140-147.

Chapter 4

AN ACADEMIC ADVISING SERVICE:
Students Helping Students

JOHN R. BONAR

C ONCEPTS and practices of academic advising in higher education have been the subject of renewed experimentation during the past decade (Bonar and Mahler, 1976; Dameron and Wolf,
1974; Lutker, 1975; Crockett, 1978; Brown, 1972). By the late
1960s students and administrators voiced discontent with the traditional faculty advising system. Students were often required to
complete a quarter or more of additional coursework in an undergraduate program because of poor or inaccurate advice from faculty advisors. At Florida State University twenty-five to thirty percent of the education majors on a typical quarterly graduation ros-
ter needed some intervention by an academic dean, either to waive
an academic requirement to insure graduation or to defer graduation until the requirements were fulfilled.

It was apparent that advising services needed improvement
along with better coordination of student services and academic
record keeping. To this end, the College of Education established a
budgeted Office of Academic Advisement and Student Services.
Its primary task was to develop a new advising program to deliver
program information to undergraduate students accurately and ef-
ficiently.

A Centralized Paraprofessional Advising Program for
Lower-Division Students

The new Office of Academic Advisement and Student Services

was established to advise 2500 undergraduates in ten departments of the college through the coordination of record keeping, admissions screening, advancement and graduation, and teacher certification. Such a centralized academic advising program was a notable departure from the earlier faculty advising program in which freshmen and sophomore students interested in education had been advised by about forty faculty volunteers (usually "volunteered" by their department heads) representing forty different interpretations of programs and regulations. These faculty received no training and were often unavailable. They frequently did not know even the requirements of programs in their own departments. Students who were undecided about a major were the most abused by this system. An advisor to an undecided student often either tried to recruit the student to his or her own discipline or ignored the student who expressed no interest in that discipline.

By contrast, the new system provided a central location where specially trained paraprofessionals could help lower-division students interested in a teacher education major develop an appropriate, balanced academic program. The paraprofessional staff were graduate students in counseling or student personnel administration with firsthand knowledge of the problems of student life. Several had had considerable work experience in these areas. Most had bachelor's and/or master's degrees in subject-matter teaching fields in education. Together, the seven paraprofessional staff provided 140 hours per week of advising time to approximately 900 lower-division students in education. The paraprofessional staff received extensive preservice training in the general academic regulations of the university, Liberal Studies (general education) program requirements, and in requirements of each degree program in the College of Education.

Each advisor spent twenty hours per week helping students, individually or in groups, develop four-year programs of study in their chosen majors. An advisor was assigned on the basis of a student's intended major. For undecided students, program planning proceeded on a quarter-by-quarter basis. Much attention was given to identifying coursework that probed their real and suspected interests. Advisors also helped students prepare their class

An Academic Advising Service: Students Helping Students 67

schedules and process any requests for changes in academic load during the early weeks of each quarter. They were regularly available for advice or referral on any aspect of a student's academic program.

Students were assigned particular advisors on the basis of intended major. They were asked to participate in group advising sessions at least once each quarter where they shared experiences with their peers. Groups and workshops (Lutker, 1975; Hutchins and Miller, 1979) have been found useful adjuncts in advising, but have not replaced one-to-one relationships. Individual advising was by appointment and involved a discussion of academic progress, program of studies, and other matters that seem best addressed in a one-to-one relationship.

Although this program focused on academic advising, the paraprofessional advisors were often involved in counseling related to vocational choices, the job market, and study skills. An extensive referral network made it possible for advisors to direct students to one of many professional counselors, for personal or social problems, and to career development resources on the campus.

A Centralized Paraprofessional Advising Program for Upper-Division Students

Because of the success of the centralized paraprofessional lower-division advising program, a similar program was instituted for all upper-division students majoring in elementary education. Academic advising in the new program shifted to trained paraprofessional graduate students paid as graduate assistants and selected on the basis of their background and experience in counseling or in the Department of Elementary Education. They helped approximately 650 students majoring in elementary education develop sound upper-division programs.

The six paraprofessionals working in this program served primarily as program coordinators working collaboratively with volunteer faculty in the Department of Elementary Education who served as professional consultants to students. Faculty were most valuable in answering questions relating to professional opportunities in the field, graduate study opportunities, and coursework equivalencies.

68 *Peer Counseling and Self-help Groups on Campus*

Like their lower-level counterparts, each was available to students an average of twenty hours per week and performed similar functions. They also processed requests for changes in academic load, provided graduation checks of academic records and helped students prepare applications for student teaching. They were regularly available for advice or referral on any aspect of students' academic programs.

Students were requested to appear for an hour's individual academic advisement with their own advisors at least once each quarter. Group advising was not used with these more seasoned students.

Computerized Management Information

The most notable difference in the quarterly cycle of activities in the upper-division program was that program management data was made available through an evolving computerized Student Information Management System (SIMS). The computerized management of an upper-division student's elementary education program began with admittance to teacher education. SIMS automated the screening process for admission to teacher education. It detailed deficiencies of those not able to pass the initial screening and periodically rescreened them. SIMS generated quarterly reports on individuals with deficiencies. Advisors were provided with biographical data after students were admitted to teacher education. SIMS then monitored students' quarterly progress as they moved through the upper-division program. SIMS determined whether students were eligible for student teaching and provided student teaching status reports to those administering the student teaching program. When students completed their programs, SIMS conducted all necessary graduation and certification checks, relieving the advisors of this tedious task.

SIMS information significantly upgraded the quality of academic advising. Paraprofessional advisors received quarterly progress reports and enrollment and academic trend analysis reports on each student. These reports noted discrepancies between planned programs and actual enrollment in classes. The reports also provided accumulated grade averages grouped in meaningful categories. Warning messages appeared automatically for students who had fallen below established academic standards. The reports also identified an individual's academic trends by comparing current and previous quarterly grade-point averages by category. SIMS also analyzed program plans of students in its data base to predict demand for individual courses.

Selection and Training of Paraprofessional Advisors

The advanced degree programs in counselor education and student personnel administration in higher education were particularly valuable sources of paraprofessional advisors. Both programs shared the view that involvement in these advising programs was a valuable adjunct to an advanced student's formal training. Potential paraprofessional advisors were identified by faculty during the admission process and a credential file with several written recommendations was submitted to the director of the advising programs. This was followed by a structured personal interview with the director, along with interviews with two or three seasoned paraprofessionals who encouraged applicants to ask any questions that they might have been hesitant to ask the program director. Each interviewer rated the applicant's responses and potential for the program using a rating scale developed for this purpose.

The final selection of advisors was made by the program director on the basis of all three elements. Those selected then went through preservice and inservice training programs. A computer-managed preservice instructional program was designed for advisors in the lower-division program. The upper-division trainees, armed with a set of training manuals, engaged in a three-day preservice orientation training session. A specially developed instrument was administered before and after training to measure mastery of advisement information. After advisors assumed their responsibilities, they attended inservice staff meetings with the Director of Academic Advisement.

The individualized computer-managed instructional program familiarized each trainee with important university and college regulations, the Liberal Studies Program requirements, and pertinent program planning considerations and helped evaluate their progress. The course could usually be completed in about three or four days of intensive participation.

The course consisted of seven "cognitive" and four "synthesis" units in booklet form. The cognitive units presented the facts necessary for making sound academic recommendations. The synthesis units were based on a number of "case studies" reflecting typical student problems. These were the heart of the course that let the trainees practice applying factual material.

After completing at least one unit, trainees reported to the Computer-Assisted Instruction Center on campus and signed on to a computer terminal. The computer presented a series of criterion-referenced evaluative items on each unit completed. If the trainees missed more than 20 percent of the items on any unit, they had to return to take a parallel test. If they did not pass 80 percent of the evaluative items on the second test, they were required to consult with the Director of Academic Advisement who reviewed the content of the unit with them before they continued their training.

Program Advantages and Disadvantages

A skilled paraprofessional advisor who is also a student in the same field can help undergraduates evaluate the pace of their progress toward a degree, balance required credits and electives, avoid the pitfalls of registration, and benefit from the experience of their peers in advisement groups. A continuing relationship with an advisor assures students that they are known and cared about by some knowledgeable person in the often bewildering university structure (Katz, 1973); since students often prefer a peer for such help, this form of counseling and advising has become quite popular (Sherwood, 1980; Upcraft, 1971).

The paraprofessionals, because of their frequent contacts with students, become unusually well-informed advisors who, as students themselves, can also relate to their advisees' problems in highly practical ways. The experience that the advisors gain in the programs is a valuable adjunct to their formal training.

There are, of course, some practical disadvantages to using paraprofessionals as academic advisors. The employee turnover rate and related training problems are significant. Beginning graduate students cannot be expected to remain in the program for more than two years. Some leave after one year to devote

An Academic Advising Service: Students Helping Students 71

more time to their graduate programs. As full-time graduate students, many find the twenty-hour a week commitment difficult, especially those with family responsibilities.

The high turnover rate creates problems. It takes time to learn all that an effective advisor must know. Students also need time to trust and develop rapport with an advisor which is difficult when advisors change frequently. Although comprehensive preservice training programs minimize the problem, fledgling advisors must be carefully monitored by administrative faculty in their early months, consuming faculty time.

All paraprofessional advisors were asked to comment anonymously and candidly on the effectiveness of the program. A representative sample of their comments follows:

(This assistantship) has been of tremendous value to me. I now have greater insight into . . . students of this age group . . . It has been a rich experience in which I have grown in countless ways.

I am seriously considering working in a junior college setting and I am sure that the experience I have had in the program will be invaluable to me if I do. The process of advisement is much different from that of counseling, and I am glad I could experience both.

Among the most valuable aspects of the program, they cited "working with students and other advisors and learning how a university operates," ". . . learning the intricacies of collegiate programs and getting to know students — their likes and dislikes." Among the most troublesome: "the clerical work and trying to fit the twenty hours a week in with my graduate program," ". . . the range of office tasks toward the latter part of the quarter," ". . . the failure of some students to show an interest."

The programs were well received by administrative and teaching faculty in the College of Education and by the wider university community too. College administrative staff even proposed a further expansion of the system. Serious consideration has been given to implementing and expanding similar programs (Bonar and Mahler, 1976) with segments of the wider campus undergraduate population, and Morrill et al., (1974) have presented a comparable program elsewhere.

The effectiveness of paraprofessional advising has been evaluated very positively in doctoral dissertations at Florida State

72   *Peer Counseling and Self-help Groups on Campus*

University through use of local assessment instruments as well as the Barrett-Lennard Relationship Inventory and the Koile Professional Activities Inventory. Similar programs have been shown to be effective on many other campuses according to reports of Brown (1974), McCaffrey and Miller (1980), and Upcraft (1971).

Guidelines for Program Replication

In conclusion, several guidelines have been developed to assist those interested in replicating this paraprofessional advising program.

1. *Establish a viable administrative structure*

To insure support for paraprofessional programs, a viable and appropriate administrative structure is essential. Because advisement is closely related to academic record-keeping, we believe it is appropriate to administer the programs through that part of the institution responsible for academic record-keeping. Beside easing access to academic records, this insures a permanent home for the program, as academic record-keeping is a necessary and continuing function of the institution.

2. *Obtain an appropriate level of authority*

Some institutional change can be brought about through persuasive argument, but sometimes program administrators must have authority to effect change. This may become critical when their changes alter faculty roles and when new advisement delivery systems disturb funding patterns or faculty autonomy.

3. *Secure adequate and consistent funding*

Competent advising costs money, and reductions in funding almost always translate into reduction of program effectiveness and services to students. When all factors are considered, paraprofessional advising is considerably less expensive than faculty advising. Funding is usually more visible and therefore more subject to cutbacks during periods of austerity. (The cost of faculty advising is rarely identified or budgeted separately and is therefore less visible.) It is very important to obtain adequate, secure funding.

4. *Identify continuing sources of potential paraprofessional advisors*

This is one way to insure program continuity. It is beneficial to establish a liaison with those academic areas that show interest and where graduate students are available with relevant previous experience and training. Their faculty provide initial screening and referral. Experience has shown that good paraprofessional advisors can come from any discipline, but some disciplines may be more appropriate than others.

5. *Develop comprehensive preservice and inservice training programs*

Paraprofessionals cannot effectively advise other students unless they know the facts on which good advising must be based. Comprehensive preservice and inservice training programs are absolutely necessary. Computer-assisted or computer-managed instruction is a promising training mechanism, especially for preservice training. The programs must be comprehensive, available at various times of the year, and require little investment of administrative time. Those programs, which are largely self-contained and individualized, minimize the involvement of the permanent staff. Inservice training can be accomplished through regular staff meetings where problems can be shared and resolved.

6. *Plan for administrative efficiency*

Converting to paraprofessional advising using centralized delivery systems means both change for faculty and students. One of the fastest ways to lose their support is to administer the fledgling program ineptly. Reassure them through efficient management practices that the programs have been carefully thought out and are operating according to plan.

7. *Effect program accountability*

Hanson (1978) urges us to plan for an accountability component as the program is designed. Measures of program effectiveness must be developed for such variables as client satisfaction, administrative satisfaction, and paraprofessional effectiveness. Instruments to obtain data must be designed and validated; their results should be available periodically to all interested parties.

Longevity is assured only through demonstrated success, and such accountability today implies cost effectiveness and cost benefit. It is necessary to know the cost of providing paraprofessional advising services and to compare it with the cost of faculty advising services in terms of the benefits to students in the two systems.

8. *Obtain adequate facilities and staff*

A program like the one described here, employing six paraprofessionals on a half-time basis, can adequately meet the advising needs of 700 to 800 students. Adequate physical facilities must be given careful consideration. The program generates heavy student traffic, so that provision should be made to insure privacy during advising sessions with a waiting area included to accommodate overflow student traffic. It is also highly desirable to provide for a permanent staff person in the facility to route students, make appointments, help with record-keeping chores and be generally available to answer questions.

REFERENCES

Bonar, J. R., & Ramsayer-Mahler, L. A center for "undecided" college students. *Personnel and Guidance Journal,* 1976, *54*(9), 481-484.

Brown, W. F. Effectiveness of paraprofessionals: The evidence. *Personnel and Guidance Journal,* 1974, *53,* 257-263.

Brown, W. F. *Student-to-student counseling: An approach to motivating academic achievement.* Austin, Texas: University of Texas Press, 1972.

Crockett, D. S. Academic advising: A cornerstone of student retention. In Delworth, U., & Hanson, G. R. (Eds.), *New directions for student services: Reducing the drop-out rate.* San Francisco: Jossey-Bass, 1978(3).

Dameron, J. D., & Wolf, J. C. Academic advisement in higher education: A new model. *Journal of College Student Personnel,* 1974, *15,* 470-473.

Hanson, G. R. (Ed.). *New directions for student services: Evaluating program effectiveness.* San Francisco: Jossey-Bass, 1978(1).

Hutchins, D. W., & Miller, W. B. Group interaction as a vehicle to facilitate faculty-student advisement. *Journal of College Student Personnel,* 1979, *20,* 253-257.

Katz, J. (Ed.). *Services for students.* San Francisco: Jossey-Bass, 1973.

Lutker, C. Academic workshop: Use of paraprofessional leaders and behavior change goals for students on academic probation. *Journal of College Student Personnel,* 1975, *16,* 162-163.

McCaffrey, S. S., & Miller, T. K. Mentoring: An approach to academic advising. Chapter 9 in Newton, F. B., & Ender, K. L. (Eds.), *Student development practices.* Springfield: Charles C Thomas, Publisher, 1980.

Morrill, W. H., Oetting, E. R., & Hurst, J. C. (Eds.). *Nine outreach programs.* Ft. Collins: Colorado State University Printing & Publications, 1974.

Sherwood, G. P. Allied and paraprofessional assistance. Chapter 16 in Delworth, U., & Hanson, G. R. (Eds.), *Student services.* San Francisco: Jossey-Bass, 1980.

Upcraft, M. L. Undergraduate students as academic advisors. *Personnel and Guidance Journal,* 1971, *49,* 827-831.

Chapter 5

PROJECT ALTERACT:
A Student Designed Drop-in and
Outreach Center

NORMAN S. GIDDAN, DONALD L. SANZ,
and MARY K. PRICE

WE wanted to develop a comprehensive, outreach drop-in center whose programs would be planned and staffed almost exclusively by student peer counselors from Florida State University. We hoped the center would illuminate and integrate several of the major tenets of campus community psychology (Banning, 1971; Caplan, 1974) including community participation in the development and delivery of services; diverse interventions at both community and individual levels such as training and referral; emergency programming; consultative and educational projects; and research and evaluation. Just as individual performance often falls short of expectation, so the reality of our center was unable to expand fast enough or develop completely enough to satisfy all of our ambitions. We did maintain an outreach orientation and were able to calibrate our programming closely to student needs and demand, to learn from evaluative feedback and enrich the project with all manner of student and campus input.

But the typical difficulties in creating a new setting (Saranson et al., 1971) were exacerbated by the inherent tension between direct counseling service and interventions aimed at campus change and prevention. Multiple types and levels of intervention

76 *Peer Counseling and Self-help Groups on Campus*

were required but did not grow easily together or live comfortably within the same center. Project Alteract developed in a stepwise fashion, almost osmotic, as it profited from reduced demand for emergency programs, moved to broader interventions like groups and training, and then incorporated social action — with campus community participation a constant ingredient. Such ingenius effort would have been admirable in a strongly supported professional mental health unit, but it was surely too ambitious where staff consisted of peer counselors and student paraprofessionals. Rather than get too far ahead of the story, let's go back to the beginning.

Project Alteract began as a drop-in educational, growth and training center, offering various personal and academic development experiences for students. During the 1970s, Project Alteract offered three major programs: (1) drop-in crisis intervention service and training; (2) personal relations training and growth groups; and (3) social action projects designed around identified unmet needs of the university population. These programs were supervised by professional staff from various disciplines associated with the University Counseling Center, which also co-sponsored Alteract with the Student Government.

PHASES OF GROWTH

Beginnings

Alteract emerged out of the student concerns surveyed and documented several years by the Office of Off-Campus Counseling for addressing social and interpersonal issues, pragmatic financial and consumer problems, and a need for human services. The Off-Campus Student Association also wanted to see a program of peer-helping-peer, along with an interest in social action projects, much like others (Hallowitz, 1968; Gartner et al., 1977), have described for community or college centers.

A Drop-in-Program

Peer Planning: It was no easy task to operationalize our goals or develop our setting. (Saranson et al., 1971). The staff (preprofessionals, nonprofessionals, and the one professional staff liaison)

Project Alteract: Student Designed Drop-in and Outreach Center 77

had to be melded into reasonable intellectual and emotional consensus on goals, policy, procedures and training. We tried to avoid using status or experience to settle disputes; emphasis was placed on a thorough, critical analysis of issues. We had to get to know each other; such a vast amount of planning required a couple of leaderless long group meetings to resolve interpersonal conflicts.

The complex combination of staff created a rewarding atmosphere, but inevitably led to diverse notions about goals and training, as well as operation of the project. We saw our task not only as providing the campus with additional skilled peer counselors but as facilitating meaningful institutional and systems reform in the broadest terms (Polak, 1971; Alinsky, 1971; Tornatzky, 1979). We found ourselves developing ideas and plans for human relations training groups not sure of our assessment of the need for them or, indeed, sure who we would be training. From the beginning we did agree on the importance of training, however, seeing it as a means of producing a legacy of trained staff and aware of its intrinsic value with relatively normal college students where outcome is often similar to that of conventional psychotherapy and counseling (Carkhuff & Truax, 1965; Cowel, 1973; Carkhuff, 1971).

In the end it was the youngest staff member who forged the policy statement that achieved reasonable staff consensus. It specified our emphasis on students learning new ways to cope and relate in an atmosphere of mutual exploration and mutual respect, on individuals taking responsibility for what they want to learn, and for the improved self-concept and willingness to take risks that can grow in such an atmosphere.

Community Feedback: After several months, certain of what we knew from our two years of surveys and evaluations, we took our remaining questions back to the University community again and banged our drum a little, too. A series of open houses, one a "Community Festival" built around a free outdoor rock concert and another by "invitation" to interested campus community members allowed us to solicit more reactions and ideas. To insure continued input from our target populations (drop-ins), we devised a feedback questionnaire to give an opportunity (not obligation) for reaction. A record of these drop-in visits turned into a demographic profile of our population, and channeled responses back into the project.

When we opened, our operating policies were as follows:

1. Staff would provide continuous coverage from 5 to 10 P.M. for crisis and drop-in services.
2. Advertising would emphasize human relations training, growth groups, and public education.
3. Development of training approaches, improved recruiting, training and selection of core staff had high priority.
4. Staff self-training would continue.
5. Crisis service would be decreased by providing planned growth group experiences led by Alteract staff or professionals from the community. If drop-in and crisis services were less necessary than expected, some conventional growth center facilities would be added.
6. Staff would provide supervision supplemented by Counseling Center faculty as required.
7. Linkages would be maintained with Division of Student Affairs, Counseling Center, Off-Campus Counseling Office and DISC.

The services of Alteract included an informal drop-in center of wider scope than most (Zapf, 1973; McCarthy and Berman, 1974; Petrillo, 1976), which was dedicated to human relations training, numerous pragmatic programs aimed at student development needs, public educational efforts such as workshops and lectures, and social action programs designed to study, to evaluate, and to propose or take action materially affecting important subsystems of the university environment. In other words, Alteract was designed to blend together personal development and growth and environmental change as has been implied or suggested by several writers, including Siegel (1973), Danish (1977), and Cowen (1973). Philosophically, individual change and social change are seen as complementary processes, each capable of influencing and shaping the other. The programs sought to develop means which foster individual growth and self-actualization along with action oriented projects (Wolff, 1974) through which each individual may draw upon his or her increased feelings of

Project Alteract: Student Designed Drop-in and Outreach Center 79

independence, creativity, and interpersonal sensitivity in order to render the environment more humane and health inducing.

Student participation ranged from one-shot Friday night "loneliness" groups to outreach for veterans, then to weekly growth groups and on to the staff training group, culminating in membership on the drop-in-house staff.

THE PROGRAMS

At the beginning, training was directed toward producing future Alteract staff members. This program concentrated on introducing future staff to (1) the operating values, the concepts, goals, sanctions and ethics of Project Alteract and (2) to the techniques and approaches of initiating, maintaining and terminating Project Alteract's "helping action processes." As the program progressed, it became apparent that more detailed staff training was needed in the areas of crisis intervention and emergency care. A training program on emergency care procedures for drug abuse (outlined in Table 5-I) was developed in order to equip staff in making skilled and knowledgeable assessments of the client's condition, appropriate referrals, and adequate liaison with the local hospital, university infirmary, and cooperating physicians in the community.

The core staff, considering the possibility that many drop-in clients might come to Alteract with drug problems, also realized that special attention should be paid to the area of drug-related crisis intervention training. In addition, paraprofessional staff received generic training related to ethical issues and confidentiality, and specific training in legal issues and counseling techniques for juveniles or offenders. One of the post-tests for the training module in what staff called "legal hassles" is reproduced as Table 5-II.

For those staff interested in further refining their interpersonal skills, a seven-session training program was designed and entitled "How to Be a Helping Person." This successful course attracted the college's students from other programs on campus including Nursing and Communications. The goals of the course included enhancing the awareness of self, increasing sensitivity to the

80 *Peer Counseling and Self-help Groups on Campus*

feelings, fears, needs, distortions, manipulations and styles involved in relating to others. Additional goals related to interpersonal relations skills such as empathy, listening, acceptance, giving and receiving appropriate feedback, and the use of feelings.

Table 5-1

TRAINING MODULE OUTLINE FOR EMERGENCY CARE OF DRUG ABUSERS

The first step that staff personnel must take in the care of a drop-in drug user is to assess his or her condition in order to decide what care is necessary. In more serious cases of drug abuse, appropriate medical assistance must be sought either by referring drug abusers to a doctor via friends, or by calling Campus Security to rush a person in dangerous condition to the Emergency Room at Tallahassee Memorial Hospital.

If a staffer assesses the drug user does not need medical attention and can best be handled by peer staffer, methods of communication and crisis intervention become especially important consideration.

This is how we see the "rough draft" of the training procedure:

I. Assessment of Condition
 A. Physical Condition — Didactic Training
 (Questions to ask yourself: Does the dropper-inner need medical care? What drug does appear to have been taken?)
 1. Symptomatology
 2. Basic skills for staffer:
 a. Blood pressure
 b. Observation of pupil response
 c. Pulse
 d. Temperature
 B. Mental Condition
 1. Training through experiential role-playing, and drawing upon the experiences of local psychiatrists and those experienced in handling drug users.
 2. Questions to be answered: Does drug user show suicidal tendencies? Is he or she hallucinating seriously? Is drug user to be handled by the staffer alone?
II. Communication with Drug User
 A. Didactic Training
 1. Terminology
 2. Lectures by speakers with experience in relating to drug users
 B. Role-playing — for staffer to become comfortable dealing with various emergency drug situations (example: dealing with "bad trips")

Project Alteract: Student Designed Drop-in and Outreach Center 81

Table 5-II

POST-TEST FOR TRAINING IN LEGAL HASSLES

I. Behavioral Objective

GIVEN THE FOLLOWING VIGNETTES, THE TRAINEE WILL RESPOND WITH 95% ACCURACY IN A WAY THAT WILL NOT VIOLATE EXISTING LAW AND WILL BE IN ACCORDANCE WITH THE STATED ALTERACT GUIDELINES.

II. Vignettes:

A. While you are on duty, a sixteen year-old girl who has run away from her home in Dothan, Alabama comes in looking for a place to crash. She says she will leave if you call her parents.

B. While you are on duty, a girl comes running in and says her boyfriend is outside in the car unconscious.

C. While you are on duty, a woman drops in and wants to know how she can determine if her teenage son is using drugs.

D. While you are on duty, a drop-in client asks what rights he has if he is arrested. He then begins telling you about a drug "score" he is going to make later that evening.

E. While you are on duty, two drunks come in and start to hassle you. They start tearing up the staff logbook and making paper airplanes.

F. While you are on duty, a girl who has been talking about trouble with her boyfriend goes in the john, closes the door. You smell grass and realize she is smoking a joint.

G. While you are on duty, a freshman comes in and says he took "some pills" to help study for finals. This is the first time he has done so and the effects of the drug are frightening him. His roommate gave him a capsule which he said would bring him "down." He wants to know if he should take it.

H. While you are on duty, an off-campus student comes in and says his landlord has locked him out of his apartment. He wants to know if he has the legal right to break a window to get in and retrieve his things.

Growth Groups

In addition to staff training and human relations training, there was at least one growth group operating at Alteract every night, Monday through Friday. Two of the staff members began a structured group for couples, an experience designed to enhance communication between partners using dyad exercises followed by group discussion of basic dialogue patterns.

Another staff member ran an Academic Improvement Group, which employed individual contracts and peer reinforcement to increase the member's motivation for academic work. Each member set a grade point average goal for the quarter and worked on weekly sub-goals.

82   *Peer Counseling and Self-help Groups on Campus*

The most unusual and probably most successful group was the Friday night program entitled "Altered States of Interaction." Members of the staff provided leadership to these informal discussion sessions, which focused on shyness, loneliness, isolation and improved social relations — appropriately ending the evening at a favorite college pub. By the end of the first year a full calendar of events included a drop-in group every night of the week and several fully enrolled groups, namely, a Personal Awareness Group, Gestalt Therapy Group, Transactional Analysis Group, Group on Future Careers, and a Gestalt Marathon weekend devoted to interpersonal exploration.

Public Education and Campus Change

Public education activities were also important to the off-campus student community. In collaboration with the Off-Campus Student Association guest lectures were sponsored that served to greatly increase the visibility of Project Alteract. Public education events also helped to expand the membership and effectiveness of the student association. In collaboration with Project Alteract, the association grew to over 200 members and served as (1) Alteract's political arm and liaison with Student Government and other university agencies, (2) the source of publicists and fund raisers for Alteract projects, (3) a recruitment resource for students interested in volunteer action, and (4) a source of student leadership. In particular, student managed social action projects (SAPS) emerged from the relationship between Project Alteract and the Off-Campus Student Association, providing a small replica of Sarason et al's., (1977) notion of resource networks. The goals of these projects were to (1) influence a subsystem of the university community toward increased fulfillment in students' lives and (2) to provide a meaningful action-oriented growth experience for the students and paraprofessional staff.

Operating decisions were based on interviews of faculty, staff, and students and on participants' reports on the problems under scrutiny. In planning, it was necessary to define the limits of the changes a SAP might reasonably be expected to make and assess its role, especially in relation to any services by existing

Project Alteract: Student Designed Drop-in and Outreach Center 83

programs or systems; whether to supplement, duplicate or work from within for beneficial change. This involved the careful assessment of problems and resources with which the change agent must begin (Alinsky, 1971); Tornatzky, 1979). Then appropriate publicity and advertising had to be framed. SAP leaders held weekly meetings to insure communication among projects and share problems and strategies, with emphasis on sharing skills, advertising and publicity. Generally, leaders and staff were trained on the job. The Social Action Projects included:

1. *Meeting People:* helping students meet each other through direct action or by stimulating this process with the help of existing organizations on and off campus. Survey findings led to (a) the revitalization of Unicorn, a nearly defunct club for single students; (b) a computerized roommate referral service and plans for a dating service in collaboration with the Computer Resources Committee: (c) informal bi-weekly get-togethers at the Project Alteract house to provide a setting in which students could relax and interact and (d) a marriage enrichment program with both experiential and didactic components.

2. *Computer Resources:* incorporating a roommate referral service, a nascent computerized dating service and "acquaintance" program to increase opportunities to meet both similar and complementary individuals.

3. *Veterans' Concerns:* locating, interviewing, and addressing common concerns of veterans within the university community. Summaries of the interviews showed a characteristic lack of group cohesion, a sense of isolation, primary concern with self and family, secrecy about veteran status, financial concerns especially related to the G. I. Bill, and heteorogeneous political views. Developed were: (a) paraprofessional training for veterans to lead rap groups devoted to their special concerns and (b) a means of locating veterans quickly to keep them informed of all possible resources and information.

4. *Residential Groupings:* setting up a "campus simulation" which reveals the location and numbers of the greatest concentrations of students; then organizing programs to help

students reach each other, on-campus services and cope with specific concerns.

5. *Creative Advertising:* communicating news of projects and ideas to the potential target group of the university comunity through a variety of print, pictorial and electronic media.

6. *Consumer Concerns:* gathering and publicizing information on costs, quality, and boondoggles of local businesses, goods, and services. Publication of a "Consumer Survival Handbook" on topics relevant to student living. Surveys on the quality of local business services and on the feasibility of a co-op have been conducted. A special task force including a consultant from a local bank set up a course in family budgeting.

ISSUES AND PROBLEM AREAS

As with most developmental programs, Project Alteract often met unexpected problems. It was difficult to recruit paraprofessionals (Sakowitz and Hirschman, 1977) with past training in crisis intervention or those known to have real potential for developing such skills. Similarly, the recruitment for faculty and community leadership was a struggle. Motivating university student participants was difficult due to other competing time demands. Our best motivational strategy was to reward students with course credit which, in turn, involved considerable efforts to modify the training programs in order to meet minimum academic expectations.

Alteract experienced the continuing problem of communicating the availability of services to the campus and local community. This process was complicated by the difficulties that students encountered in finding the drop-in-program. Considerable time and effort was devoted to advertising, which included contacts with classes, departments, university and community groups, and appearances at any function where a large number of students congregated. In addition, funding was a continuous problem. Begun with virtually no funds, Project Alteract continued to survive through the support of the University Counseling Center and a small materials grant from the Student Government.

Accountability: Alteract was successful in developing a student-run, student-oriented alternative to traditional counseling and social action programs. Programs and projects were developed on the basis of documented student needs. The evaluation process included drop-in session feedback forms, diaries kept by student leaders, statistics on the number and type of program participants, and staff meeting minutes. In the first six months, for example, 633 participants were identified, including drop-in clients, group members, and staff. This count did not include student participants in public education events such as lectures by visiting experts, films, TV shows, and staff presentation to larger campus audiences. The combined attendance at these groups and public presentations exceeded one thousand persons. Concurrently, the Off-Campus Student Association reached a membership of two hundred students. Another sign of success was the degree to which Project Alteract staff were called upon to deliver training workshops. For example, University Orientation involved seventy student volunteers hosting visiting freshmen to talk in small groups about personal concerns and problems and generally to offer support, help, and encouragement during this transition period.

One important means of evaluation was to document staff changes over time. The experience of taking an idea and putting it into action to develop a new setting had its usual frustrations. But staff members rapidly began to develop a staying power and a philosophical attitude toward adversity that crystallized in one meeting when it seemed that no funds were available and the drop-in house might be lost. Many staff members were sustained by a deepening commitment to future careers in the helping professions. This was fostered by their growing confidence in delivering meaningful services. Their abilities became evident in their academic work, as several members received graduate credit for Alteract participation. Other students structured parts of their peer experience to meet requirements for a particular course. A systems analysis of the project, for instance, was performed for a "systems" course, and several training modules were created for academic credit. Evaluating Alteract and its processes was yet another learning experience, as was couching the evaluation reported here. Staff found special talents and skills that they had in program development. For example, plans to train student academic advisors for the dorms and for veterans developed as a direct outgrowth of the Academic Improvement Groups. This continuous discovery of latent staff talent was a dynamic and rewarding process that Project Alteract helped to elicit.

Our experiences led us to reflect on much that has been written during the past fifteen years about the beauty and the necessity of the community mental health concept, although considerably less has been written about how to implement it. Simply and briefly stated, the community approach is important because it best serves and involves the most people. Theoretically, it could contribute to the well-being of everyone. Efforts supposedly focus on primary intervention designed to eliminate the sources of potential problems before they materialize, as opposed to waiting for the problem to occur and then offering remedial treatment to the afflicted individual. Thus the emphasis of the community approach may rest upon development of human potential rather than exclusively upon curing mental dysfunctions. Actually including these community concepts in the creation of a multipurpose campus peer counseling center has been a remarkable learning experience for us, marked by challenge, change and cooperation, and guided by a renewed respect for reality.

REFERENCES

Alinsky, S. D. *Rules for radicals: A practical primer for realistic radicals.* New York: Random House, 1971.

Banning, J. H. Campus Community mental health: A model and status report on western campuses. Paper presented at the meeting of the American Psychological Association. Washington, D. C., September, 1971.

Caplan, G. *Support systems and community mental health.* New York: Behavioral Publications, 1974.

Carkhuff, R. R., & Truax, C. B. Training in counseling and psychotherapy: An evaluation of an integrated didactic and experiential approach. *Journal of Consulting Psychology,* 1965, *29,* 333-336.

Carkhuff, R. R. Principles of social action in training for new careers in human services. *Journal of Counseling Psychology,* 1971, *18* (2), 147-151.

Cowen, E. L. Social and community interventions. *Annual Review of Psychology,* 1973, *24,* 423-472.

Project Alteract: Student Designed Drop-in and Outreach Center 87

Danish, S. J. Human development and human services: A marriage proposal. In Iscoe, I., Bloom, B. L., & Spielberger, C. D. (Eds.), *Community psychology in transition.* New York: Haworth Press, 1977.

Gartner, A., Riessman, F., & Jackson, V. C. *Paraprofessionals today. Vol. 1: Education.* New York: Human Sciences Press, 1977.

Hallowitz, E. The role of the neighborhood service center in community mental health. *American Journal of Orthopsychiatry,* 1968, *38,* 705-714.

McCarthy, B. W., & Berman, A. L. A student-operated crisis center. Chapter 2 in Zimpfer, D. G. (Ed.), *Paraprofessionals in counseling, guidance and personnel services.* Washington: APGA Press, 1974.

Petrillo, R. Rap room: Self-help at school. *Social Policy,* 1976, *7*(2), 54-58.

Polak, P. Social systems intervention. *Archives of General Psychiatry,* 1971, *25,* 110-117.

Sakowitz, M. L., & Hirschman, R. Paraprofessional selection: Myth or safeguard. *Journal of Community Psychology,* 1977, *5,* 340-343.

Sarason, S. B., Zitnay, G., & Grossman, F. K. *The creation of a community setting.* Syracuse, New York: Syracuse University Press, 1971.

Sarason, S. B., Carrol, C., Maton, K., Cohen, S., & Lorentz, E. *Human services and resources networks.* San Francisco: Jossey-Bass, 1977.

Siegel, J. M. Mental health volunteers as change agents. *American Journal of Community Psychology,* 1973, *1,* 138-158.

Tornatzky, L. A guide for the indigenous change agent. Chapter 7 in Alley, S. R., Blanton, J., & Feldman, R. E. (Eds.) *Paraprofessionals in mental health.* New York: Human Sciences Press, 1979.

Wolff, T. Helping students change the campus. *Personnel and Guidance Journal,* 1974, *52,* 552-556.

Zapf, R. F. Rap shack: Using volunteer counselors. *Personnel and Guidance Journal,* 1973, *52*(2), 105-108.

Section II
SELF-HELP STRATEGIES

Chapter 6

ORGANIZING AND LEADING
WOMEN'S SELF-HELP DISCUSSION GROUPS

MARY P. TYLER

THE Women's Discussion Group Program grew out of the conviction that there needed to be a forum (Lieberman and Bond, 1976; Norman, 1976) for discussing the issues surrounding contemporary feminism for university-affiliated women. Women working with the Florida State University Counseling Center developed the program after we became aware that university women must carry out their own developmental tasks in the context of strong, subtle, and painfully contradictory social expectations. For example, since she opened her first picture book, the woman student has been bombarded with images of the ideal woman as pretty, passive, and somewhat incompetent. Yet in her classes, she is expected to be logical, persistent, and intellectually productive. If she decides to enter one of the responsible professions for which her education prepares her, she will find it necessary at times to advocate for her own position in an assertive manner. Yet such behavior is likely to be labeled as "strident" or "threatening" when aspiring towards academic professional success, which is frequently perceived as hindering a woman's chance for marriage. Women uninterested in marriage are perceived as mildly neurotic, contributing to what Horner (1970) describes as the "fear of success."

Women who are married students with or without children or are married to student-husbands face a unique set of social pressures. Such women are either postponing the development of their own intellectual interests until their husbands complete their studies or are pursuing their education in an environment with minimal supports (Bardwick, 1971).

The lack of self-confidence engendered by such a social climate tends to isolate women from one another. Since socially approved roles and behaviors for "women" and "people" are often divergent or even mutually exclusive, it is difficult for a woman to perceive herself as both an adequate woman and an adequate person. One way of justifying her seemingly inadequate existence is to denigrate women who have different life-styles. The fulltime mother can criticize the working mother for neglecting her children; the graduate student can call the housewife "boring." Consequently, women often avoid serious interaction with one another and tend to devalue other women's ideas and opinions. The results are demoralizing. An inability to value a group to which one belongs can only decrease self-esteem. A lack of opportunity to compare one's problems with those of other women can lead to the erroneous interpretation that one's difficulties are the result of purely personal failings according to Silverman (1972).

The behavior of women in various roles is also subject to a psychological "double standard." It has been shown that even sophisticated mental health workers express quite different expectations for a "healthy woman" and a "healthy adult" (Schaffer, 1981; Broverman et al., 1970). Normal women are seen as lacking independence and aggressiveness, as illogical, subjective, and passive. This stereotypic definition of feminity is particularly incongruent with the values of the university, where rationality, persistence, and independent achievement are respected and rewarded. The young woman learning to function in the university community finds no coherent set of expectations to which she can conform. Instead, any pattern of behavior that she adopts will be subject to some degree of criticism or disrespect.

Searching for a Response

As we considered the destructive aspects of the university community, we also saw that some women manage to emerge

Organizing and Leading Women's Self-help Discussion Groups 93

from this environment as strong, self-confident individuals. We began to analyze the attitudes and behaviors involved in such strengths in order to organize a women's self-help program led by paraprofessionals that could instill these traits in a larger group of women. The following four major goals emerged as we watched women respond to some beginning discussion group experiences:

1. An awareness of the environmental forces impinging on women so that the participant can understand her own experiences in their social context.
2. An ability to understand herself in the light of feminine sex-role socialization, recognizing both the aspects of herself that she truly values and the aspects that are unnecessary or maladaptive responses to women's socialization.
3. Motivation to put her new understanding into action by experimenting with new ways of being herself and interacting with her environment.
4. A sense of affection and respect for other women together with a capacity to give and receive emotional support in relationships with other women.

Developing a Program

Considering the breadth of these goals, our structure would seem deceptively simple to a casual observer. Several groups of ten to twelve members and two professional or paraprofessional co-leaders began meeting for two hours a week during a nine-week academic quarter. The style of the gathering was informal; the women sat in a circle on the floor and talked together. At the beginning of each session a leader usually distributed discussion materials. At the end of the discussion, members spent a few minutes writing brief statements about their reactions to the meeting.

Though the group format had much in common with that of a consciousness-raising group (Eastman, 1973), the differences reflected a commitment to provide the most extensive developmental experience possible within the limited time frame of the academic quarters. Since the traditional relationship between a woman and a professional group leader can perpetuate the feelings of inadequacy and powerlessness (Chesler, 1971); Schaffer, 1980),

94   *Peer Counseling and Self-help Groups on Campus*

being "helped" by a leader in a group experience could have the same deleterious effect. Therefore, in order to avoid the slow pace of unstructured group process, the following meeting format was developed to accelerate group movement without restricting members' control over their experience: (1) including a mixture of women in each group so that each woman can meet a variety of others; (2) the use of optional discussion materials; and (3) a leadership style which minimizes the differences between the roles of leaders and members.

The Members

Since one of our goals is to enhance the members' capacity to like, respect, and seek out significant friendships with other women, we consider it important that the others with whom they share the group experience represent the widest range of lifestyles. We believe that breaking the usual pattern of avoiding "different" women can help participants feel better about themselves as women and widen the range of people that they might turn to for companionship. Though drawing from the university population imposes a degree of homogeneity, a group typically includes women from nineteen to forty-five years of age with a variety of occupations and educational backgrounds. Initially demographic differences are seen as potential barriers, but as members get to know each other they are usually surprised to learn that they have much in common and a great deal to offer each other.

To ensure a varied membership, members are recruited in several ways: word-of-mouth publicity from former members, the school newspaper, staff newsletter, married student housing newsletter, or university radio and television stations. For some it is one of several possible projects for courses in the social sciences. Others are referred by the counseling center staff as an adjunct to individual work. For example, a woman's group could help a woman going through divorce feel more confident about beginning to function as an independent, unmarried woman. In other situations, the self-help group experience alone may be the most appropriate referral, as in the college student groups developed by Pierce and Schwartz (1978).

The Discussion Materials

At the beginning of each meeting the leaders introduce discussion materials, usually mimeographed excerpts from books or articles presenting several points of view on a topic of interest to women, but not required for discussion. Members read the materials quickly and bring up any aspects they would like to discuss. Usually much of the discussion is related in some way to the topic, but members also bring in other issues. The materials have two purposes. One is to ensure that members give at least passing thought to a wide range of issues that are relevant to the lives of contemporary women. Second, the sequencing of the materials is important to help move the group toward the goals of the program.

The materials for the first two meetings help participants get to know each other and discover that they share many experiences, feelings, and ideas. The first are a set of hypothetical situations: "Your instructor rarely calls on women in class and never seems to notice when you raise your hand. What do you do?"

In the second meeting each member gives a five-minute autobiography. This step in getting acquainted builds group solidarity and begins a process of learning to like other women. When members begin to compare experiences, several kinds of sharing take place. There is a nostalgic warmth from learning that everyone loved Nancy Drew mysteries and a shared resentment of the agonies that resulted from the high school popularity cult. As the closeness of shared feelings and experiences develops, various women begin to exhibit qualities that earn the respect of their peers, such as having a fresh insight on an issue. Comments written after meetings express surprise and pleasure at discovering such admirable qualities in other women.

The third and fourth meetings introduce more focused topics for discussion. The stimulus materials for the third meeting are a stack of representative read-aloud books for preschool children. In many, bumbling little girls cry over their mistakes or look on while boys have adventures. Fewer are interesting stores about likeable, admirable girls or women. After the women look through the books, the discussion usually turns to the general topic of sex-role socialization, both as a social issue and as an influence on the lives of the participants. The materials for the fourth session include another set of hypothetical situations and a handout on "Approval" which presents some of the ideas about conflicting expectations for women.

The third and fourth sessions are also usually marked by a shift from a simple awareness of social problems to awareness coupled with a motivation for change. It is important that this occur fairly early in the group's development. Becoming aware of the social and personal injustices experienced by women can be very painful. Discovering with the group's support that it is possible to affect these conditions provides women with a constructive channel for anger and frustration. The shift toward an activist orientation can usually be seen in a comparison of the way hypothetical situations are discussed in the first and fourth sessions. In the first session such situations usually elicit a sense of shared experience and feelings of indignation. In the fourth, they provoke more statements like "Next time somebody asks me to bake cookies for a party, I'm going to say I'd rather set up the stereo."

Members begin to bring in reports of experiments with new ways to approach situations. One group's reaction to the children's books was to explore their concepts of themselves as mechanically inept and their tendency to unload repair jobs on males. "After all," exclaimed one member, waving a book about a clever boy craftsman in the air, "we all know they've been fixing things since they were five years old!" The next week there were reports of repairing a porch and a toaster, and beginning a serious study of the VW engine. All these accomplishments were praised by other women and there was an excited sense of wondering what other tasks might actually be feasible.

The next four sessions are introduced by handouts on "Marriage," "Sexuality," "Achievement," and "The Legal and Economic Status of Women." During the week before the session on sexuality, members read the book *Our Bodies, Our Selves.* As the topics introduced by the readings are discussed, the conversation tends to become more focused and deeper than in earlier meetings. Personal concerns are discussed in the light of their social context, and solutions are explored in terms of both personal behavior and social change. Some women report that they have rarely pursued a point to its logical conclusion or felt comfortable arguing a position with any force. Apparently the group differs from social situations in that seriousness or willingness to argue are not defined as unfeminine. It differs from school or work situations in that there is no threat of being evaluated or having to compete. Recognizing a capacity to talk seriously and effectively without dire consequences seems to be important in enhancing the self-esteem of many participants.

The group's cohesiveness becomes increasingly intense during the last few minutes. Discussion of termination is usually accompanied by sadness, but there is also enthusiasm about plans for new kinds of experiences, such as joining women's organizations or taking women's studies courses. The last meeting, which is devoted to an activity planned by the group, differs from one group to another. One group went out to a neighborhood tavern and had a grand time — it was the first time many of the members had gone out in public with a group of women. Another group wrote to state legislators then debating the Equal Rights Amendment, a new experience of political activism for many. Each activity symbolized a feeling of self-confidence and sisterhood that had grown out of the group experience.

The Co-leaders' Role

The role of the co-leaders has been difficult to conceptualize. However, as we have struggled toward clarification of a leader's functions, the appropriateness of paraprofessional leaders for the program has become apparent, just as Barrow and Hetherington (1981) have found in other groups. As we began to define our role as leaders, we strove to avoid any style that implied that the leaders "had it all together" while the members were struggling. We did not see the traditional helper-helpee or teacher-student models as making an optimal contribution to the participants' feelings of self-worth and autonomy. Fortunately we were all so embroiled in our personal struggles with issues related to feminism that none of us had to combat any illusions of the wise enlightening the ignorant. True to our feminine socialization, we found it more difficult to recognize the positive things we had to offer the groups. We came to see ourselves or other group leaders as women who were working toward the same goals we had set for group members — an awareness of self and society, a capacity for bringing about constructive changes, and a sense of affection and respect for other women.

We decided that our greatest contribution to the groups would be in our attitudes and behaviors, which by serving as models, could help them attain these goals. Therefore, the leaders' behavior is essentially an attempt to do what we would like the members to do, a manner of influence characteristic of self-help groups according to Gartner and Riessman (1977). For example, the leaders, by bringing in their own concerns and ideas model a willingness to trust other women and respect their opinions. As the discussion progresses, a particularly difficult type of interaction may be introduced such as arguing about an issue. A warm emotional climate is conveyed which facilitates trust and openness. Other members also contribute to the group in all of these ways. The main differences are that the leaders are more likely to introduce behavior patterns earlier than members of the group might do, and they act as back-up in case no one else makes a needed intervention.

This role-sharing also applies to traditional leadership functions, such as insuring that no one is ignored or treated disrespectfully. During a fast-moving discussion, a shy member might venture an opinion tentatively and be overlooked as more assertive members direct the discussion. Typically the leader would wait to see if the woman reintroduces her point or if another member leads the discussion back to it. If not, the leader might say "Jane, I was interested in what you were saying about cooperative day care. Do you think that would work on this campus?" This response differs from what most of us learned to do as leaders of various kinds of counseling groups; here the leader does not confront or interpret one member's difficulty in talking or the others having overlooked her ideas. Instead she supports the hesitant member's attempt to contribute to the discussion and models a mode of attending and reaching out to others.

There are several reasons for limiting leaders' behaviors to those that would also be appropriate for members. Since the group

Organizing and Leading Women's Self-help Discussion Groups   99

is designed to enhance feelings of autonomy and self-esteem, it is important for each member to feel that she can exert her fair share of influence. It is also important for members to be exposed to patterns of interaction with which they can choose to experiment inside or outside of the group. Thus leaders try to behave in ways that would be appropriate in most interpersonal settings. Traditional leadership functions, such as directing the course of a discussion or responding helpfully to another person's concerns are important in a wide range of social situations. Consequently it is important that members have the chance to develop their abilities to perform these tasks. Such experiences are often especially meaningful discoveries of personal competence. One member wrote, "I couldn't believe that anyone had even taken note of what I had said, let alone thought about it and had it change their life. It was the greatest feeling!"

Selection and Supervision of Paraprofessional Leaders

The overlap between the behavior of leaders and members makes the program particularly well suited to paraprofessional leadership. Potential group leaders are selected throughout the quarter. Each quarter, leaders observe and identify a few group participants who reflect a skill and capacity to be open about themselves, sensitive to other people, and able to interact in helpful ways. Such women are invited to serve as group co-leaders the next quarter. When possible, a new leader is teamed with one who has previously led a group. As a former member begins to serve as a leader, her change in role is subtle. She still introduces issues of personal interest and responds to other members as she did in her previous group. But, she begins to feel more responsibility for the progress of the group and to give more thought to ways in which each member's experience could be enhanced. She does not, however, need to learn a new style of responding to people; she continues to develop the commitments and interpersonal skills she originally brought to the program.

Supervision for leaders is collaborative and nonhierarchical. It is assumed that each leader has something unique to contribute to the others. A leader with extensive mental health training and experience in leading other types of groups may be adept at unraveling the dynamics that led a particular session to an impasse. On the other hand, one who is not conditioned by responding in another mode, such as an encounter group, may find it easier to think of appropriate ways to respond in difficult situations. Each participant can help others understand the special concerns of different groups of women, such as students, working mothers, housewives, divorcees, and women of various ages and cultural backgrounds. Paraprofessional leaders are able to develop consultative skills by helping colleagues work with a problem, deciding whether information, analysis or emotional support would be most helpful. Discovering ways in which she can facilitate the work of other leaders, including those more highly educated or more experienced than herself, can be important in enhancing her sense of personal competence.

Peer supervision of leaders occurs in two settings. One is an informal, post-group meeting of the co-leaders who read the members' feedback sheets, compare reactions to the meeting, and talk over any unresolved issues or interpersonal tensions that may need to be dealt with in the next meeting. They exchange feedback when it is needed and discuss ways in which as a team they might approach members or issues in the following session. This is also a time for sharing frustrations or rejoicing at progress. Leaders also have a weekly luncheon meeting at which previous leaders are also welcome. This meeting serves several functions. We can compare the reactions of our groups to the past week's materials and explore any need for changes. Co-leaders can bring up issues that caused them special difficulty. Exploring these together, we usually learn more about ourselves and women in general. For example, discussing the problem of how to cope with a member who dominates the conversation has led us to explore our own feelings of discomfort about confronting another woman with our displeasure at her behavior. A general issue has been the role of the leaders, such as how much responsibility we should take for various group functions. Our working definition of the leaders' role evolved out of such discussions. The meetings are long enough also to allow time to talk about whatever we are interested in or simply to enjoy being together.

The leaders' group serves as an outlet for any of a leader's concerns which do not seem appropriate to the group she is

Organizing and Leading Women's Self-help Discussion Groups   101

currently leading. A leader struggling with the question of whether the oppression of women can be eliminated without revolutionary social and political change might find that concern met with open-mouthed silence in the group struggling with the idea that men might share some responsibility for housework. A more immediately interested and sympathetic audience of such radical ideas might be found in the leaders' group.

After being in two or three groups with the same structure, leaders find that they can no longer feel genuinely enthusiastic about discussing topics they have already dealt with. They have new concerns which are difficult to share with their groups or have become more interested in working actively for change than in discussing problems. Consequently most leaders eventually move on to other kinds of experiences, such as organizing women's studies courses, working with a rape crisis center, or working for political changes. This turnover is essential to the program. New, enthusiastic, leaders must be recruited regularly, since effective modeling cannot occur if the leader is not sincerely interested in the group's discussion. Though paraprofessional leaders usually remain with the program only for about a year, most find that the experience is one step in a series of increasingly challenging and empowering endeavors. The confidence and concern for other women that grows out of group leadership can help prepare women for activities which, at one time, might have seemed too frightening or demanding.

Program Evaluation

The evaluation of the program had two aspects, a session-by-session analysis of group process and an analysis of the overall impact of the program on participants. The study of process was based on a content analysis of members' weekly feedback sheets and leaders' session evaluation forms, and on the leaders' comparison of experiences at each weekly meeting. During the first two quarters, these observations were used mainly to improve the discussion materials, timing of topics, and other structural aspects of the program. For example, after discussions of sexuality proved to be difficult and uncomfortable, we discovered that placing the topic late in the series and introducing *Our Bodies, Our Selves*

102   *Peer Counseling and Self-help Groups on Campus*

as additional discussion material resulted in more comfortable and meaningful conversations. We learned that some memorable selections, such as those from Simone de Beauvoir's *The Second Sex* (1952), were written in a style too complex to be dealt with adequately in a quick presession perusal. Selections from popular writers that introduced similar ideas but were more easily absorbed were more useful in eliciting discussion. After the format stabilized, session-by-session observations led to the formulation of group process described above.

The analysis of overall impact began with a simple questionnaire containing such items as "Has participation in this group had any effect on your feelings about yourself?" Answers tended to be consistent with the program's goals. Members reported having become more confident, more aware and proud of being women, more inclined to like other women, and more insightful about themselves and their environment. The responses of one group of thirteen women to an administration of the Counseling Services Assessment Blank (Hurst and Weigel, 1968) at the end of a quarter suggested that they felt positive about the group experience. For example, on a five-point scale ranging from "extremely negative" to "extremely positive," the mean response to the question "How would you rate your total overall counseling experience" was 4.53. Leaders were rated 4.62 and members 4.15 on a five-point scale ranging from "very helpful" to "of no help at all." On questions about the confidentiality of information disclosed in the group, with a rating scale ranging from 1 for "blabbed all over campus" to 5 for "strictly confidential," members received a 4.82 mean rating, leaders a 5.00.

The preliminary outcome evaluations suggest that members leave the group with a positive feeling about the experience and the belief that they have experienced the kinds of changes that the program was designed to bring about. These evaluations are in accord with many other reports on self-help in the literature (Caplan and Killilea, 1976; Katz and Bender, 1976). However, our data are open to the criticism of having been drawn from self-report measures. Since participants responded anonymously, the results gave the leaders confidence that most members actually do leave the experience with good feelings about the group, their leaders, and fellow members.

REFERENCES

Bardwick, J. *Psychology of women.* New York: Harper & Row, 1971.

Barrow, J., & Hetherington, C. Training paraprofessionals to lead social-anxiety management groups. *Journal of College Student Personnel,* 1981, *22,* 269-273.

Beauvoir, S. de. *The second sex.* New York: Knopf, 1952.

Boston Women's Health Book Collective. *Our bodies, our selves.* New York: Simon & Schuster, 1973.

Broverman, I. K., Broverman, D., Clarkson, F. E., Rosenkrantz, P., & Vogel, S. R. Sex-role stereotypes and clinical judgments of mental health. *Journal of Consulting and Clinical Psychology,* 1970, *34,* 1-7.

Caplan, G., & Killilea, M. (Eds.). *Support systems and mutual help.* New York: Grune & Stratton, 1976.

Chesler, P. Patient and patriarch: Women in the psychotherapeutic relationship. In Gronick, V., & Moran, B. K. (Eds.), *Woman in sexist society.* New York: Basic Books, 1971.

Eastman, P. E. Consciousness-raising as a resocialization process for women. *Smith College Studies in Social Work,* 1973, *93,* 153-192.

Gartner, A., & Riessman, F. *Self-help in the human services.* San Francisco: Jossey Bass, 1977.

Horner, M. S. Femininity and successful achievement: A basic inconsistency. In Bardwick, J. M., Douvan, E., Horner, M. S., & Gutmann, D. (Eds.), *Feminine personality and conflict.* Belmont: Brooks Cole Publishing Co., 1970.

Hurst, J. C., & Weigel, R. G. Counseling services assessment blank. Fort Collins: Rocky Mountain Behavioral Science Institute, Inc., 1968.

Katz, A. H., & Bender, E. I. *The strength in us.* New York: Franklin Watts, 1976.

Lieberman, M. A., & Bond, G. R. The problem of being a woman: A survey of 1700 women in consciousness-raising groups. *Social Policy,* 1976, *7*(2), 363-379.

Norman, J. Consciousness-raising: Self-help in the women's movement. Chapter 16 in Katz, A. H., & Bender, E. I. (Eds.), *The strength in us.* New York: Franklin Watts, 1976.

Pierce, R. A., & Schwartz, A. J. Student self-help groups in a college mental health program. *Journal of College Student Personnel,* 1978, *19*(4), 321-330.

Schaffer, K. F. *Sex-role issues in mental health.* Menlo Park: Addison-Wesley, 1980.

Schaffer, K. F. *Sex roles and human behavior.* Cambridge: Winthrop, 1981.

Silverman, P. R. Widowhood and preventive intervention. *Family Coordinator,* 1972, *21,* 95-102.

Chapter 7

SELF-HELP RAP GROUPS AND PEER COUNSELING IN THE GAY COMMUNITY

MICHAEL B. SCHWARTZ

THE helping professions have undergone a revolutionary change of perspective regarding services for homosexuals in recent years (Lenton, 1980; Enright and Parsons, 1976; Gibbs and McFarland, 1974). The view has been challenged that homosexuality by itself is symptomatic of pathological processes, and with it the view that homosexuals as a group should be "treated" for their sexual preference. Instead, the prevailing weight of professional opinion seems to have moved toward the view that homosexuals constitute a mixed group of both well and poorly adjusted individuals of whom only a minority require treatment (Hoffman, 1968; Weinberg, 1973). In fact, a significant proportion of the mental suffering of gays is believed by many to be attributable to the prevailing public attitude of revulsion and hostility towards them, codified in criminal law and institutionalized in discriminatory practices in employment, housing, law enforcement, and other areas.

Indeed, it has been suggested that proponents of the pathological view of homosexuality may have been unknowingly contributing to the suffering of those whom they were attempting to help by providing the public with an easy rationalization for its discrimination against and rejection of homosexuals.

Self-help Rap Groups and Peer Counseling in the Gay Community   105

This recognition has given rise to a new philosophy in the treatment of homosexuals who have mental and emotional disorders; namely, gay patients who wish to do so may be helped to make a better adjustment *within* their sexual preferences. The recognition that the proportion of homosexuals who are emotionally disturbed may not be significantly greater than that of the general population and that homosexuals may have certain problems in common arising out of their status as a rejected minority may have stimulated the development of new counseling and support programs which do not seek to change a person's sexual preference.

This chapter describes one attempt to meet some of the developmental and social needs of a small group of homosexuals using the social group work and the peer counseling methods, under the auspices of a university counseling center.

The Gay Peer Counseling Program at Florida State University was developed in part by a small group of students who were members of the Gay Liberation Front. Several GLF students initiated a series of meetings with the staff of the FSU Counseling center in which they presented a number of pointed questions regarding the treatment of gay students who applied for counseling. Some of these questions involved the willingness of counselors to accept gay clients who wanted help in functioning better as homosexuals, or within their own sexual orientation. Other questions involved counseling that might be given to "closet cases," homosexuals who had not acknowledged either to themselves or to others the nature of their sexual preferences. There was a sincere interest on the part of the gay community in modifying existing programs and creating new ones to meet their specific needs. A beginning program emerged out of a small gay rap group which had been initiated by interested social science professors.

The structure of the Gay Program evolved from the dual interests of its members in maintaining both a Gay Rap Group and a Gay Peer Counseling Service. The program was open to all members of the community, not just university students and faculty. An individual could refer himself or herself after: (a) hearing of the program through local radio or TV interviews; (b) reading advertisements in the "personal" column of the university newspaper; (c) referral by community mental health

106   *Peer Counseling and Self-help Groups on Campus*

professionals who had been informed of its existence by briefings and through listings of community resources; or (d) by consulting the Telephone Counseling Service. The program coordinator generally interviewed each applicant briefly to determine needs and to assign the individual to one or more activities within the program. One of the important reasons for this initial professional screening was the reluctance of peer counselors and Gay Rap Group members to have contact with individuals whose needs and interests had not first been professionally evaluated.

In the screening session the individual was given a choice to participate in any one of the following activities: (1) recipient of one-to-one Gay Peer Counseling; (2) membership in the Gay Peer Rap Group; or (3) gay peer counselor in training. Each of these roles was explained and the individual was given the opportunity to choose and discuss his choice of activities. Generally this mutual selection process worked well.

The Gay Peer Counselors' training sessions were held each week just prior to the weekly Gay Rap Group in which all of the gay peer counselors also participated. During the first year, approximately fifteen individuals participated in gay peer counselor training and about half that number continued long enough in their training (at least six weeks) to qualify for providing one-to-one Gay Peer Counseling. Approximately fifty individuals received one-to-one peer counseling. More than 200 individuals attended the Gay Rap Group.

Gay Rap Group

This group was conducted so as to give maximal responsibility for its direction to the group members themselves, with interventions (Sata, 1974; Katz, 1970) aimed primarily at encouraging democratic decision-making, mutual support and acceptance, and other self-help qualities. Thus the group had relatively little formal structure imposed by its facilitator and was able to evolve through several critical stages of the group development.

There were periods of expression of deeply felt need on the part of many group members for greater closeness and sharing of feelings and concerns. There were opportunities for many group members to express their sense of alienation and isolation from

Self-help Rap Groups and Peer Counseling in the Gay Community   107

the straight (nonhomosexual) world and to express their frustration at the frequent failure of the local gay community to provide a wholly adequate alternative. There were glowing accounts given of the complexity and sophistication of the gay subculture in larger cities. There were periods in which there was considerable discussion of relationship problems of individual members. When these problems were related to the member's relative inexperience within the gay subculture, the group often gave considerable support and helpful advice. However, when the nature of the problem was common to most homosexuals, the trend of the discussion was often toward exchanging information (National Gay Task Force, 1979; United Presbyterian Church, 1978) and intellectualization. Topics which tended to recur were:

1. The relative paucity of social life in the local gay community.
2. The probability of long-term homosexual relationships being successful.
3. The question of homosexual promiscuity.
4. Problems regarding parents' and relatives' attitudes towards one's homosexuality.
5. The question of whether it is possible for an individual to be truly bisexual and the suspiciousness of some exclusive homosexuals.
6. Problems related to selecting a career and finding and keeping a job.
7. Discrimination against homosexuals by the dominant culture.
8. Medical problems peculiar to homosexuals.
9. Problems in sexual functioning (from both qualitative and quantitative standpoints).
10. People in public life known to be homosexual.
11. Problems in accepting variations in homosexual behavior which many felt gave homosexuals a "bad reputation" such as pedophilia, the "T-room trade," and the exhibitionistic "screaming queen."
12. Problems in relationships between male and female homosexuals.

13. Various homosexual meeting places such as gay bars and and public baths and the difficulties that many members had in dealing with these places.
14. Problems related to "coming out" and acknowledging one's homosexual orientation.
15. Problems involving the decision to disclose or conceal one's homosexual orientation from straight employers, coworkers, teachers, parents, siblings, and others.
16. Problems that homosexuals have in identifying other homosexuals in various social situations.
17. Difficulties in finding both acceptance and self-acceptance as a homosexual within various religions and religious sects.
18. Problems generated by the emphasis placed upon physical attractiveness by much of the gay community.
19. Difficulties in establishing contact with the homosexual community after recent arrival in an unfamiliar city or school.
20. Fears that a small group of morbidly psychopathic individuals might hurt or abuse homosexuals.

It is possible to gather from this selected list of topics that social problems are more prevalent than individual psychological problems. It is this fact that makes the social group work method, with its emphasis on group support and concerted group action to solve common problems, so relevant. As Konopka (1963) has noted, the key elements of social group work are:

1. Addressing the *psychological* maturation of the individual in the context of *social* maturity by educating the individual to function effectively and democratically within a group and within the community.
2. Providing a mechanism by which individuals may work together to help themselves through *changing their environment,* as well as themslves.

The Gay Rap Group discussed many of these common concerns and debated the feasibility of various courses of social or political action aimed at environmental change such as the Sidels (1976) suggest. Such a dialogue often brought to the surface

Self-help Rap Groups and Peer Counseling in the Gay Community   109

much of the fear, resignation, and fatalism that many, especially the older, homosexuals felt regarding the prospects for effective collective social action. Nevertheless, the group did participate in various social action activities including planning and conducting a number of homosexual social events on campus, planning and participating in a local television interview program that devoted forty minutes to homosexuality, and attempting to "integrate" a straight disco lounge that discouraged gay attendance.

The Gay Rap Group served a number of different functions within the small local homosexual community, not all of them anticipated. Partly because it accepted new members on a continuous basis, it served as a point of socialization within the gay community. Individuals from out of town occasionally entered the group as their first point of contact with the gay community. The group was also used to make announcements of information important to the gay community. It is possible that individuals who subsequently became sexually involved with one another may have first met through the Gay Rap Group, no less than might be the case with any similarly sized heterosexual group.

The fact that the group always remained open to new members, some of whom did not remain with the group for more than a few sessions, tended to create a schism between the "regulars" who were with the group since its inception and the newer members. The regulars tended to feel somewhat inhibited in being emotionally open and making self-disclosures in the presence of a shifting membership. This problem was partially resolved by earlier members impressing upon newcomers the confidentiality that is expected of them, and also by the fact that most of the regulars also met separately as peer counselors.

The discussion themes alternated between the self-disclosure of personal feelings and discussions of films, literature, research findings involving homosexuality, useful information, and humorous stories. These periods of mutual supportiveness facilitated cohesiveness in the group. It is believed that this experience strengthened the group's and its members' abilities to function socially through providing a kind of refuge for gay people from the stresses of both the straight world and the social world of the gay community itself.

Gay Peer Counselors

The gay peer counselors comprised a subgroup of individuals from within the Gay Rap Groups who made themselves available for consultation to: (a) individuals seeking to learn more about their own sexual identity; (b) university classes in medicine or the social sciences; and (c) various community groups wishing to learn more about homosexuality.

The philosophy underlying the gay peer counseling program was based upon the recognition that much of the stress that homosexuals encounter is related to their membership in a rejected subculture. Therefore, rather than providing primarily psychotherapeutically oriented counseling, the gay peer counselor engaged in sharing the kind of subculture-specific social skills and knowledge that are required to be able to function within a stigmatized, outcast social group. Some of the specific issues and questions with which students and peer counselors struggled were:

1. How does a person decide that he or she is, or is not, homosexual?
2. How does one look more deeply into the nature and origins of one's current sexual conflicts, short of extensive psychotherapy?
3. How does one establish contact with other homosexuals?
4. Does the peer counselor engage in sexual relations with those he or she counsels?
5. If the individual has engaged in a small number of homosexual contacts, is he or she destined to become exclusively homosexual?
6. How should homosexuals prudently control the flow of public information about their own sexual orientation?
7. Which factors determine how successful and popular one will be within the homosexual community?
8. What are the various subgroupings within the homosexual community?

Many of these questions call for the kind of information best supplied by an individual with direct personal experience.

The gay peer counselors met weekly with the Project Coordinator for training and discussion of their cases. The training

Self-help Rap Groups and Peer Counseling in the Gay Community   111

was a two-way process, with peer counselors contributing to the Project Coordinator's knowledge of the gay community, while he attempted to provide rudimentary training in principles of interviewing, establishing a helping relationship, and making effective referrals. Because of the relatively small number of counselors in the group, it was possible to gear training to the individual needs of each counselor. This individualized training had several other advantages. It provided continuous feedback to the trainer about the needs of the target population. It reduced the anxiety of the trainees by providing early successful experience in a previously unfamiliar activity. The experiential nature of the clients' needs and concerns seemed to make a more lasting impact on the trainee than the traditional didactic approach to training.

The peer counselors were a very mixed group of individuals, ranging in age from early twenties through late forties. They also showed considerable variation in emotional maturity and life experience. However, the few volunteers who seemed to lack maturity tended to select themselves out in the training process. One dramatic example was an individual who resigned in protest that he was not permitted to have sex with counselees as a method of fully orienting them to homosexuality.

The Nature of Peer Counseling

In general, it seemed that the peer counselor's greatest asset was that ignorance about psychodynamics helped to prevent the counseling relationship from taking on the formality of a professional relationship. It is for this reason that the mental health professional needs to guard against the impulse to train volunteers in his/her own professional "image." It may be useful to conceptualize the peer counselor as having some unique characteristics or capacities which the professional does not, owing both to different life experiences, and to the constraints that are peculiar to the professional therapeutic relationship (Gershon and Biller, 1977). These constraints include: (1) the usual prohibition on self-disclosure by the professional psychotherapist; (2) the exclusive focus upon the needs and feelings of the patient or client; (3) the focus on searching for hidden or obscure meanings to everyday experience; (4) the therapist's avoidance of the role of instructor or provider of useful specific information; and (5) the lack of time, as well as inclination, to engage in everyday social discourse. However, the ability to engage in normal social discourse, the ability to instruct, the time to deal in detail with current reality at the surface level, the freedom to emote more-or-less spontaneously and to discuss one's own past were all available to the peer counselor as long as he or she was encouraged to make use of them.

The peer counselors were in many respects regarded as experts rather than trainees and the coordinator served as consultant rather than instructor. It was found early in the program that the peer counselors had a good knowledge of conscious coping mechanisms required to contend with the difficult world of the homosexual and were quite willing to share enthusiastically their expertise with others. Where they needed the most help was in discovering and appreciating their "natural" talent, dealing with anxieties about their lack of professional training, recognizing that small inadvertent errors were not likely to do irreparable damage, and that their abundant natural human compassion, unfettered and more-or-less spontaneously applied, was their most valuable gift and their most potent tool.

This is not to suggest that some of the basics of the counseling relationship were not utilized. Some of the concepts found most useful were: (1) attentive and empathetic listening; (2) maintenance of client autonomy; (3) avoidance of proselytizing for a particular point of view; (4) counselor availability in time of crisis; (5) appropriate and effective referral and follow-through for services beyond the capacity of the counselor; and (6) responsibility for planned termination or transfer when necessary.

The types of client who availed themselves of the Gay Peer Counseling Service are easily divided into two categories. The first group of individuals were those who had sought counseling in relation to some aspect of the "coming out" process. This group included individuals who were in conflict about even giving serious consideration to accepting a bisexual or homosexual identity and individuals who had decided to do so and required only the means to become assimilated. Of those individuals who appeared undecided about their sexual identity, approximately

Self-help Rap Groups and Peer Counseling in the Gay Community   113

one-half decided in the course of their counseling *not* to identify themsleves as homosexual. Their decisions seemed to be the result of a lengthy process, often several years, that culminated in their counseling experience. In this regard the peer counselors were cautious not to proselytize for the homesexual life-style but to present a candid, balanced picture of its burdens as well as its pleasures. Even if the peer counselors were to have been heavily biased in favor of homosexuality, their influence could only represent a small fraction of the pro-heterosexual, anti-homosexual conditioning each of us receives in the dominant culture.

The second major group was comprised of individuals who had already established some identification with the gay subculture but were having difficulty functioning in some major adult social role, such as their career, family, or school. Some of these individuals had a history of psychiatric care and/or had been withdrawn and isolated not only from the straight world but from the functioning homosexual world as well. Casual and superficial homosexual contacts may well have constituted the closest affectional ties that they were able to tolerate. In such cases, the ongoing relationship with the gay peer counselor served as a link with reality and as an exposure to real human acceptance in the face of the individuals' double stigma as both homosexual and emotionally disturbed. In all these cases, the peer counselor worked with the Project Coordinator when needed to make appropriate referrals to the Gay Peer Group, to the University Counseling Center, or to other mental health agencies. The peer counselor was the referral link described by Hesse (1976).

The Gay Program functioned mostly with male homosexuals, although some females had attended both the Gay Rap and the peer counselor training group. The relative lack of participation by females seemed attributable largely to the fact that there was a Lesbian Rap Group associated with the Women's Center on the university campus. There was also some loss of interest on the part of female counselor-trainees because of the very small number of females seeking one-to-one gay peer counseling services in contrast to the larger number who seemed to be more comfortable attending group rap sessions.

It became evident in the course of individual peer interviews as well as in discussions held by the Rap Group that only a small minority of the approximately 250 individuals who had contact with both elements of the program had any history of psychiatric treatment including either hospitalization or outpatient psychotherapy. Therefore, it appears that the gay program was able to establish contact with a group of individuals who, for reasons including the lack of available treatment resources or fear of rejection, might otherwise not have had exposure to either spontaneous or organized professional help with their social or emotional problems.

In discussing with the gay peer counselors their reasons for volunteering for this kind of work, there was a recurrent theme that seemed to sum up the philosophy of both the Gay Peer Counseling and Gay Rap Group programs. These individuals had, in their own lives, undergone long periods of imposed stress and turmoil while deciding to become identified with a feared, hated, and outcast subculture. It was their purpose, individually, and the purpose of the Gay Programs to do everything possible to alleviate this unnecessary suffering for others.

REFERENCES

Enright, M. F., & Parsons, B. U. Training crisis intervention specialists and peer group counselors as therapeutic agents in the gay community. *Community Mental Health Journal,* 1976, *12,* 383-391.

Gershon, M., & Biller, H. B. *The other helpers: Paraprofessionals and nonprofessionals in mental health.* Lexington, Mass.: Lexington Books, 1977.

Gibbs, A., & McFarland, A. Recognition of gay liberation on the state-supported campus. *Journal of College Student Personnel,* 1974, *15*(1), 5-7.

Hesse, K. A. F. The paraprofessional as a referral link in the mental health delivery system. *Community Mental Health Journal,* 1976, *12,* 252-258.

Hoffman, M. *The gay world.* New York: Bantam Books, 1968.

Katz, A. H. Self-help organizations and volunteer participation in social welfare. *Social Work,* 1970, *15*(1), 51-60.

Konopka, G. *Social group work: A helping process.* Englewood Cliffs, N. J.: Prentice-Hall, 1963.

Lenton, S. M. A student development response to the gay issue. Chapter 13 in Newton, F. B., & Ender, K. L. (Eds.), *Student development practices.* Springfield, Ill.: Charles C Thomas, Publisher, 1980.

National Gay Task Force. *Twenty questions about homosexuality.* New York: Author, 1979.

Self-help Rap Groups and Peer Counseling in the Gay Community 115

Sata, L. S. Group methods: The volunteer and the paraprofessional. *International Journal of Group Psychotherapy*, 1974, *24*, 400-408.

Sidel, V. W., & Sidel, R. Beyond coping. *Social Policy*, 1976, *7(2)*, 67-69.

United Presbyterian Church. *Blue book one, 190th General Assembly*. San Diego: Author, 1978.

Weinberg, G. *Society and the healthy homosexual*. Garden City, N. Y.: Anchor Books, 1973.

Chapter 8

A CARING COMMUNITY ON CAMPUS

GARY J. FALTICO

THE myth of the university as an ivory tower often disguises a campus community whose pressures may separate students from one another or catalyze the confusion in their interpersonal relationships. In this frantic period of their lives, what might have been a community of growth may provide only temporary and fragmented contacts with others.

For many students, college is the first stage of emergence from the protected environment of family and traditional life-styles on the way to the heavy privilege of independence. The opportunity to explore new ideas and relationships can lead to identity confusion as they explore definitions of self and confront new choices.

Students in the late 1960s and 1970s seeking some counteractive force to these pressures involved themselves with everything from drugs to radical politics to self-help modalities (Keniston, 1965; Nahal, 1971; Hunter, 1972; Bloom, 1975; Gartner and Riessman, 1977). Increasingly they rejected traditional models and methods to experiment with new approaches to personal, social, and vocational identity. The forms of these experiments were not always easily integrated with the structures, practices, and policies of academic institutions. During the past two decades shrinking membership in sororities and fraternities, diminishing participation in student government, and declining levels of school spirit have alarmed student personnel administrators concerned with the students' preoccupation with self.

A Caring Community on Campus

In response to these challenges and needs in the student community, a unique residential program was developed on the campuses of Florida State University and the State University of New York at Purchase. Known as the Caring Community, it was made up of students who had participated in encounter and human relations groups sponsored by the counseling services of the college and individuals strongly motivated toward deeper involvement in relationship building. The program was rooted in three approaches to personal and interpersonal growth: (1) the communal movement, (2) the therapeutic community model of treatment, and (3) Glasser's concept of the Community Involvement Center.

The communal aspect of the Caring Community was attractive to students who had lived in communes before coming to college and students who wanted to experience a positive and structured communal environment. Others, who had participated in more structured communes with political or religious themes, welcomed this opportunity to build their own commune on a college campus. The last group of students was curious about the nature of communal living as an alternative to the college dormitory.

Therapeutic community is a concept of treatment and rehabilitation which has been well described elsewhere (Bassin, 1968; Casriel, 1971; Gartner and Riessman, 1977). Such therapeutic communities as Daytop Village, Synanon, and DISC Village, as well as the prototypic Alcoholics Anonymous, share a goal of responsible concern for each other. They utilize the unique insights and motivations of the ex-addict to help others overcome their own destructive and irresponsible patterns of behavior.

This aspect of the program's model discouraged some prospective members. Confrontation sessions, encounter groups, the "Synanon games" and techniques borrowed from Daytop Village alienated some individuals with backgrounds atypical of Daytop members and for whom drug abuse was not a personal concern.

Glasser has extended his concepts of Reality Therapy from the psychiatric hospital to the educational system and now to society as a whole with the concept of a Community Involvement Center (Glasser, 1965, 1969, 1972). Based on the assumption that cooperating individuals can pool their talents and resources

118   *Peer Counseling and Self-help Groups on Campus*

to provide for each other with needed services, Glasser noted the human need for cooperation and affiliation could be enhanced in a growth-oriented Caring Community that promoted human learning and mental health rather than failure and anxiety.

The Caring Community Facilities

The campus Caring Community designed to provide peer counseling and social services was first housed in one wing of a four-floor dormitory building. Living arrangements included suites for eight persons sharing a bathroom and small study and a wing of six double and two single rooms whose fourteen occupants shared a bathroom and a television lounge. The Project Director (author) lived in a faculty apartment in the same wing, next door to the lounge of the Caring Community corridor. By the second semester, twenty new members made it necessary to branch out into two more suites and an additional corridor on other floors of the same building, a physical separation which resulted in some communication difficulties.

The design of the building facilitated this kind of group program. The suites and study areas lent themselves to small group meetings. There were kitchenettes to prepare occasional meals. In the first semester our closeness gave us immediate access to each other, resulting in an open door atmosphere.

The corridor/suite arrangement allowed coeducational wings throughout the dormitory. The Caring Community began with eleven female and six male members, the same ratio as the campus in general. As the program expanded, dormitory counseling staff were housed in the faculty apartments, which helped extend Caring Community's contact to other staff and other student areas in the dormitory. As a new residence hall, it was plagued by delays in furniture delivery and disrupted utility service. Though some other students reacted with anger, frustration and damage to the building, the Caring Community shared in the necessary service and maintenance responsibilities.

Organizational Roles and Functions

The Caring Community began with an organizational structure similar to that of Daytop Village (Bassin, 1968). As we found

A Caring Community on Campus 119

that members could not relate to many of Daytop's techniques, we worked toward a more flexible and democratic model fitted to the needs of responsible college students, a model that enhanced communication and growth. The organizational structure that emerged is described in Figure 9-1.

The structure of the Caring Community included indirect relationships (shown by dotted lines) through the residence counselor to the Dean of the Division of Student Affairs and the Residence Hall staff administration. The Project Director was also the Director of Counseling Services for the College, and was directly responsible to the Dean of Student Affairs. The goal of the Project Director was to facilitate the development of the Caring Community's own resources for organizing and administering programs to a point where it could operate without faculty and staff direction.

A counseling intern served as the Coordinator of Group Leader Training for the program and did double-duty with public relations and liaison service responsibilities. She conducted experiential and didactic training sessions for peer group counselors and co-led a number of "human potential" groups with Caring Community members. Each component of the program was chaired by a student volunteer who was accountable to the Caring Community and the Project Director.

The chair of the Service Crew assigned weekly housework duties to all members, who were expected to spend about forty-five minutes a week cleaning the shared, public areas of the community. Except for special training needs, the overburdened college maintenance and housekeeping staff did not come into this area. The result was an environment cleaner and more attractively decorated than any other area of the dormitory. Beyond this obvious responsibility, the Service Crew experience provided opportunities to evaluate attitudes and relationships.

The Group Leaders Program involved peer counseling in a human potential group format. The chair of the Food Program was responsible for purchasing food and assigning duties connected with potluck Sunday suppers and such other events as the Community occasionally sponsored. (The Community's regular meals were provided along with the other residents of the dormitory.) The chair of the Finance Program functioned as a treasurer, maintaining the Caring Community checking account and disbursing petty cash.

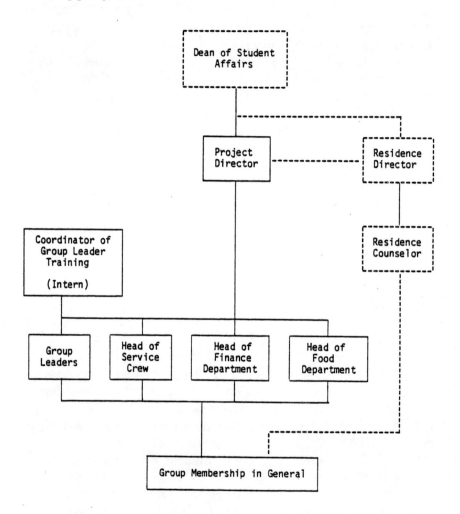

Figure 8-1. Organizational structure for the Caring Community.

It would have been more efficient to assign one person to a given role for the entire academic year, but rotations in some of these positions provided more meaningful and diverse learning experiences. As in a therapeutic community, work assignments in the Caring Community offered a challenge, provided learning experience, and avoided deterioration into a sterile routine.

The work of the various departments was evaluated by the group membership. Sometimes chairpersons were criticized in group meetings for using their authority arbitrarily or neglecting their responsibilities to challenge those who failed to carry out responsibilities.

At first, group problems were resolved by group consensus, but as the program expanded and its locations multiplied, it became impossible to set meetings that all members could attend. Decision making required a voting process, generally carried out by posting memoranda on a central bulletin board with sign-up sheets to poll opinions on topics of common importance.

Development of Open Admissions Policy

Initially the screening and selection of members included the completion of a questionnaire and an interview. The questionnaire requested background data and reasons why the individual wanted to join the Caring Community. A group of items were included to survey the strengths, limitations, and general outlook of the applicant. Half-hour individual interviews were used to orient the applicant to the goals of the Caring Community and to answer questions. Many of the reasons cited for wanting to join the community included: (1) an opportunity to meet people (66%), (2) to become more open and honest (55%), (3) to help others (44%), and (4) to humanize the college (33%).

After extensive contact with the first group of members, it was decided that acceptance into the Caring Community should be based on both individual and group decisions and that tests and interviews should be employed primarily for orientation so that every student who applied would be accepted. When the time requirements of residential participation became clear, some students with severe time limitations were permitted to live in their own homes or in other sections of the dormitory and to attend only certain groups that the Community sponsored.

The general selection policy of the Caring Community was that anyone could contribute and gain something. This open (and revolving) door policy had both advantages and disadvantages for the organization of the community as some members contributed more than others.

Peer Counseling and Self-help Groups on Campus

The experience was enriched by the membership of at least one representative of every division of the college. Backgrounds and interests were diverse. Certainly the disorganization, confusion and conflict that can result from diversity also impinged occasionally on program objectives, but generally the program was enriched, and the open admission policy continued.

Orientation Program

The orientation program for new members was rooted in sensitivity or human relations training and encounter group formats. Early in each semester, the group went on an extended weekend training retreat. New members were introduced to the Community through campus marathons which adapted some of the microlab techniques of William Schutz (1971) and other encounter group techniques (Rogers, 1970; Stevens, 1973).

This kind of intensive orientation to self-expression and group involvement resulted in positive and enthusiastic feelings and gave new members a feeling of closeness to a large number of people in the very first week. For many, these groups sowed seeds of friendship which matured with time and shared experiences. The emphasis on nonverbal encounter techniques enhanced feelings of camaraderie and reduced some of the barriers to communication. One general meeting at the beginning of each semester presented the practical, business, and scheduling aspects of the program.

The orientation emphasized the involvement of experienced members in welcoming and acclimating new members to the program, a familiar component in self-help according to reports in Caplan and Killilea (1976) and Bratter's (1974) paper.

Voluntary Group Opportunities

The Caring Community emphasized group involvement, the essential mediating environment of self-help Katz and Bender (1976) tell us. All of its members were encouraged to participate in at least one group a week if their schedule permitted. The four forms of ongoing voluntary group activity included the morning meeting, encounter groups, the seminar, and the general meeting.

The *Morning Meeting,* held each weekday for about forty-five minutes before classes, was divided into announcements, "pull-ups and push-ups" and a segment aimed at waking up and starting the day positively. Following announcements of the day's activities and requests for volunteers, individuals confronted the group with positive or negative reactions to events of the previous day. A "pull-up" is a negative confrontation with the purpose of exploring the attitudes behind behaviors, like asking whether members were beginning to lunch only with other Community members, projecting an in-group image to the campus. "Push-ups" provided thanks, recognition, or approval, like "Thanks to all of you who took care of me when I was sick last night." This was a unique aspect of the Caring Community program in contrast to the pull-ups and confrontation in a therapeutic community. This daily mechanism was designed for expressing feelings that might have hardened into grudges in other living situations on a college campus. The meeting ended with theatre games, singing, yoga, or some sensory awakening experience for starting the day. Members shared leadership of the Morning Meeting, volunteering for a day or a week, discussing plans with members and inviting candid feedback. Thus it served as an informal group leaders' training.

Several *Encounter Groups* met weekly. Some members chose to be part of ongoing encounter groups while others attended occasionally for help in dealing with unresolved conflict. Complaints could be filed by "dropping a slip" in an encounter box naming the problem and the individuals involved. Those who dropped slips were encouraged to verbalize their feelings at the beginning of meetings with assistance provided by giving feedback on here-and-now feelings.

Encounter group meetings also provided an opportunity to train leaders. Many of the encounter group principles and procedures were drawn from Mowrer's (1972) concept of the Integrity Group, the Peer Self-Help Psychotherapy Group described by Hurvitz (1976), and the Ivey (1971, 1973) Microcounseling process. After gaining some experience in the Caring Community, counseling interns assumed roles as co-leaders and supervisors of peer group leaders. The theories and techniques used in these groups have largely come from the human potential literature (Rogers, 1970; Schutz, 1971; Stevens, 1973).

A third type of group, *the Seminar,* consisted of a brief discussion of a general theme primarily as a means of exploring the reactions and interpretations of all the members. These were often included as parts of other meetings and usually limited to fifteen or twenty minutes. The discussion began with the leader stating a topic or quotation of interest to him or her, a personal reaction, and an invitation to others to respond. In the round-robin that ensued, each member had the chance either to interpret the "seminar statement" or to pass.

General Meetings were topic-centered and called whenever a significant number of people believed that an issue warranted consideration by the entire community. They were like town hall meetings where all members were encouraged to express their opinions and decisions were reached by democratic process. As it became increasingly difficult to schedule general meetings due to conflicting time schedules, meetings were shortened and increased in number to permit the maximum number of members to attend.

Campus Involvement

The Caring Community established a goal of demonstrating a positive role in the life of the campus in order to prevent a meaningful living situation from being viewed as an exclusive project. Therefore, members sought contacts with other campus groups in order to share the opportunities of the Community with others. For example, a group of Caring Community members volunteered to work with other students on the campus as "orienters," helping freshmen and transfer students as they arrived. They provided services ranging from carrying baggage to offering advice and companionship during the advisement and registration processes, extending the peer approach as Wolff (1974) and Holbrook (1974) have. Their presence definitely improved the atmosphere and efficiency of the orientation program. Its success prompted the college to consider using orienters at an even earlier stage in the admissions process.

The Group Leaders Training Program became a second outreach activity by providing all interested students an opportunity to learn about and experience group dynamics. Our approach had much in common with other peer counseling (Bishop and Sharf, 1972; O'Donnell and Oglesby, 1978; Hutchins et al., 1976) training for residence hall support personnel. Five members of the Caring Community met weekly to discuss readings on group dynamics and encounter group techniques, explore the ethics and responsibility of group leaders, and develop plans for student-run human potential groups. In role play the trainees worked through a number of group issues and interactions, serving as both members and leaders of this specialized group. Concurrently, the trainees served as co-leaders of ongoing human potential groups. The training group served as a peer supervision session involving the Counseling Services intern and their peers in helping to plan and evaluate their own groups.

The Caring Community participated in two training programs for peer counseling projects in other school settings. At the invitation of the directors of high school peer-counseling training, members demonstrated role playing and led discussions of the responsibilities of peer counselors and the techniques that they might use on one-to-one crisis counseling. They also demonstrated small group counseling techniques and a reality therapy model of peer interaction.

Two members of the Caring Community submitted a proposal to the Psychology Department and to the Division of Student Affairs for establishing a peer counseling training program in relationship to a hot line and crisis center for the campus. Their proposal, based on experiences within the Caring Community and visits to a number of peer counseling programs in other colleges and universities, was subsequently considered as a basis for a credit course in peer counseling techniques.

In addition, members of the Caring Community made presentations at a number of professional meetings including the American Psychological Association, the Association for Humanistic Psychology, and the American Personnel and Guidance Association meetings.

Another outreach project sponsored by the Caring Community was a campus clean-up campaign. At least one day a week, Caring Community members distributed garbage bags to students as they left the lunchroom and shared in a campaign to pick up the trash

126   *Peer Counseling and Self-help Groups on Campus*

throughout the campus. Beyond improving the appearance of the campus, the shared activity seemed to have a positive effect on the attitudes of many in the wider community toward both the Caring Community and the campus.

The general atmosphere and activities of the Caring Communities provided ongoing outreach opportunities through such unstructured and spontaneous events as potluck meals, musical happenings, and car pool trips to New York. Many visitors remarked on how the open door atmosphere contrasted with other sections of the dormitory. Perhaps this was the essence of the Caring Community and its primary contribution to the lives of those within and around it.

Critical Issues and Problems

As the program emerged from its initial confusion and dependency on the director for day-to-day leadership and grew toward autonomy and self-government, conflicts were increasingly resolved between the members involved. Peer-sponsored human potential groups met regularly with new methods and language replacing the essentially borrowed language of therapeutic communities. Perhaps most positive and important, the Caring Community has grown strong enough to provide outreach to the campus.

There were, of course, areas where improvement was still needed. For some members of the Caring Community other interests, priorities, or requirements led to decreased involvement. Attendance at peer sponsored encounter groups fell off towards the end of the academic year and group participation in general appeared to suffer with the advent of examination and term project deadlines.

There was some unresolved faculty concern. A few faculty members reflected some concern that the Caring Community might inhibit the growth of its members whereby intense group involvement might become an excuse for a student not to function in other spheres of his or her life. In fact, we knew that in cases where students neglected their contacts with nonmembers or appeared to be sliding in their academic responsibilities, the group expressed its concern and encouraged the individual to evaluate and modify his or her behavior. The intensity of group pressure and the impact of peer approval seemed to vary with the person. For some, participation in encounter and other group sessions increased dependence. However, these problems surfaced early in the orientation to the Caring Community and the combination of self-selection to membership and peer support helped each individual make appropriate adjustments.

Some of the college staff feared that the group's influence might be put to "political use." In fact, the membership of the Caring Community did not participate in student activist programs, indeed, nor have a united policy toward dominant political issues on or off the campus. This was unlikely, given the diversity in this community. More effective public relations with college staff about the actual goals and functions of the Caring Community might have dispelled such fears.

Student opinion concerning the value of the Caring Community experience was divided. Some nonmembers perceived the program as cliquish. Yet others, affected by alienation elsewhere, sought ways to become involved in the activities of the Community.

In conclusion, it is important to return to Glasser's concepts of Reality Therapy, which emphasize the importance of *involvement* in all growth processes. He identifies mutual investments of attitudes, ideas, energies and feelings as raw material for successful educational and personal change, a concept permeating many new self-help and peer programs reported by Nash et al., (1978). A constructive environment of confrontation appears to offer the ideal atmosphere for such growth. Various groups, which emphasize responsibility in peer relationships and assessment of one's own behavior, can contribute significantly to the maturing self-concepts of their members (Caplan and Killilea, 1976; Katz and Bender, 1976). This occurs in situations where the options available to the participant are success rather than failure, reward rather than punishment, and achievement rather than frustration.

It appears from even a preliminary evaluation of the Caring Community that Glasser's principles apply to the college experience as well. It is important, furthermore, that the diversity of

128   Peer Counseling and Self-help Groups on Campus

individual backgrounds, talents, interests, and life-styles be respected in the development of collegiate programs of this sort. A community involvement program in which differential talents are put to use to achieve multiple goals through the shared participation and involvement of diverse individuals and groups seems an appropriate and valuable model for the development of Caring Communities on any campus.

REFERENCES

Bassin, A. Daytop village—stopover or cure? *Psychology Today*, 1968, December, 48-52.

Bishop, J. B., & Sharf, R. S. A helping relationship course for residence hall advisors. *Journal of College Student Personnel*, 1972, *13*, 462-463.

Bloom, B. L. (Ed.). *Psychological stress in the campus community: Theory, research and practice*. New York: Behavioral Publications, 1975.

Bratter, T. E. Reality therapy: A group psychotherapeutic approach with adolescent alcoholics. In Seixas, F. A. (Ed.), *The person with alcoholism*. New York: The New York Academy of Sciences, 1974.

Caplan, G., & Killilea, M. (Eds.). *Support systems and mutual help*. New York: Grune & Stratton, 1976.

Casriel, D. H., & Amen, G. *Daytop: Three addicts and their cure*. New York: Hill & Wang, 1971.

Gartner, A., & Riessman, F. *Self-help in the human services*. San Francisco: Jossey-Bass, 1977.

Glasser, W. *Reality therapy: A new approach to psychiatry*. New York: Harper & Row, 1965.

Glasser, W. *Schools without failure*. New York: Harper & Row, 1969.

Glasser, W. *The identity society*. New York: Harper & Row, 1972.

Holbrook, R. L. Student volunteers as helpers in residence halls. Chapter 4 in Zimpfer, D. G. (Ed.), *Paraprofessionals in counseling, guidance, and personnel services*. Washington: APGA Press, 1974.

Hunter, R. *The storming of the mind*. Garden City: Doubleday, 1972.

Hurvitz, N. The origins of the peer self-help psychotherapy group movement. *Journal of Applied Behavioral Sciences*, 1976, *12*, 283-294.

Hutchins, D. E., Yost, M. W., & Hill, D. E. A comparison of undergraduate and professionally trained head residents. *Journal of College Student Personnel*, 1976, *17*(6), 504-510.

Ivey, A. E. Demystifying the group process: adapting microcounseling procedures to counseling in groups. *Educational Technology*, 1973, February, 27-31.

Ivey, A. E. *Microcounseling: Innovations in interviewing training*. Springfield, Ill.: Charles C Thomas, Publisher, 1971.

Katz, A., & Bender, E. *The strength within us*. New York: Franklin Watts, 1976.

A Caring Community on Campus 129

Keniston, K. *The uncommitted.* New York: Harcourt, Brace & World, 1965.

Mowrer, O. H. Integrity groups: Principles and procedures. *The Counseling Psychologist,* 1972, *3*(2), 7-33.

Nahal, C. *Drugs and the other self.* New York: Harper & Row, 1971.

Nash, K. B., Jr., Lifton, N., & Smith, S. E. *The paraprofessional: Selected readings.* New Haven: Advocate Press, 1978.

O'Donnell, W. J., & Oglesby, C. L. Paraprofessional counselor training for residence hall personnel. *Journal of College and University Student Housing,* 1978, *8*(2), 25-26.

Rogers, C. R. *Carl Rogers on encounter groups.* New York: Harper & Row, 1970.

Schutz, W. C. *Here comes everybody.* New York: Harper & Row, 1971.

Stevens, J. O. *Awareness.* New York: Bantam, 1973.

Wolff, T. Undergraduates as campus mental health workers. Chapter 4 in Zimpfer, D. G. (Ed.), *Paraprofessionals in counseling, guidance, and personnel services.* Washington: APGA Press, 1974.

Chapter 9

SELF-HELP TRAINING OF
STUDENT COUNSELORS FOR OVERSEAS
EDUCATION PROGRAMS

MARY P. TYLER and DONALD L. SANZ

AN unusually challenging request for a paraprofessional
training program was made to the Florida State University
Counseling Center by the coordinator of FSU's overseas study
centers. Seeing a need to improve student personnel services for
undergraduates studying in the London and Florence centers,
he asked for assistance in selecting and training the graduate
students who serve as their counselors. In each center three
counselors live in a hotel with approximately eighty undergraduates for a six-month term. The counselors take extensive responsibility for personal counseling, program administration,
and both educational and recreational programming.

When we agreed to develop a selection and training program
for these individuals, we realized there were some unusual problems. Most of the graduate students had no interest in exploring
the helping professions or in developing their counseling skills
for future professional work. A typical team of student counselors
might include doctoral students in archeology, art history, and
philosophy. Though our selection procedure enabled us to choose
counselor trainees who had the potential ability to take leadership, plan programs, and serve as paraprofessional counselors, the
trainees had not yet developed these skills to any great extent.
The typical trainee was more apt to inquire about the distance

Self-help Training of Student Counselors for Overseas Programs   131

from the hotel to the nearest museum than to ask whether the center had an adequate file of mental health referral sources. Not only did we see a need to reorient the counselors' priorities and introduce them to new ways of thinking about their roles, we also realized that we were training them for an unusually complex and demanding set of responsibilities (Sue, 1973; Pedersen et al., 1976; Vontress, 1969, 1971).

The three counselors in a center would be the only student personnel or mental health workers in the setting. Access to professional consultation and referral resources would depend on the counselors' own ingenuity. They would need, for example, to become acquainted with local health facilities in London or Florence. Since faculty rotate through these centers on a six-month basis, counselors could not usually expect a great deal of guidance from faculty members. Though the directors were more experienced in the settings, the complexity of their responsibilities made it unreasonable to expect that they could devote much time to supervising the counselors. In addition to taking on a number of difficult, unfamiliar tasks with little supervision, the counselors would be required to function even when they were under severe personal stress. Stumbling off the crowded chartered airplane, they would be as exhausted and overwhelmed as the undergraduate students who would be looking to them for strength and guidance.

As we thought through these problems, we realized that we were attempting to prepare a group of intelligent but inexperienced people to take on heavy responsibility under personally stressful circumstances in the absence of significant backup or supervision. Further, because of a number of practical constraints, we had available only five evenings of contact with the trainees. If we were to have a significant impact, we would need to devise a training program far more efficient and intense than anything we had previously attempted. In attempting to produce dramatic emotional and cognitive changes in a brief period of time, we combined techniques used in intensive weekend growth groups with those typically used in paraprofessional training programs described by D'Augelli and Danish (1976).

The Paraprofessional Trainers

Our first consideration in organizing a training program was the selection of paraprofessional trainers. In order to maintain a one-to-one trainer to trainee ratio, we needed six trainers. Having a fairly large group of trainers allowed us to include a diverse group of people, some with organizational skills, others with individual and group counseling expertise or with experience in living abroad. Our trainers needed to be skilled in their areas of expertise and able to work with inexperienced students in a demanding training situation. Since we wanted trainers who could apply existing competencies to a novel set of problems, we recruited undergraduate and graduate students who had been trained in other paraprofessional programs. Students who had served as trainers for the Telephone Counseling Service were experienced in peer counseling and peer counselor training. Those who had worked with Project Alteract and the Off-Campus Student Association were well grounded in program development and group leadership skills. As we were able to pay the trainers only a small honorarium, it was important to find people who would give their services in return for a personal learning and growth experience. Consequently most of the trainers had career aspirations in the various helping professions. Their sophistication and the experimental nature of the program led to a high degree of paraprofessional involvement in structuring the program as suggested by Allen (1974). Their contributions added a wealth of practical experience and good ideas while giving them opportunities to explore the new role of program designer. Their role in actual training sessions was the same as that of the co-authors; thus in describing the program, we will use the term "trainer" to refer to all of us.

The Structure of the Program

There were four training sessions of two to four hours each, and one large group meeting that included the participants in the foreign studies programs that served as the "final exam" for the training experience. We devoted most of the first session to training in one-to-one counseling skills. Our first problem was to engender motivation to learn counseling skills in individuals who had

Self-help Training of Student Counselors for Overseas Programs   133

never given much thought to the importance of listening, considering feelings, and other ways of relating (Levy, 1976) that make peer counseling somewhat different from other kinds of interaction. To do this we began the session with an exercise that came to be known as the "scare wheel." In this the trainees sat in a circle, each trainee facing one trainer, the trainer role-played a problem likely to occur in the foreign environment and asked the trainee for help. Each role-playing situation lasted three minutes. Then the trainee moved on to the next trainer, who presented another problem. After each trainee had dealt with six different problems and attempted to help in some way, we called time and discussed the trainees' feelings and needs at the moment.

At this point we invariably found that the trainees felt overwhelmed and inadequate. We helped them understand that while we weren't expecting them to be psychotherapists, we would be able to train them to deal in a productive way with problems of these kinds. We also stressed that they had been chosen for this program because of their potential for handling such situations. At this point their motivation to learn was at a high level. We then went into more intensive role-playing situations, the trainers giving feedback where appropriate and at times changing roles with a counselor to illustrate how a problem could be dealt with. We drew these role-playing situations from a master list of problems compiled from interviews with returned students and counselors from these programs. Some of the role-playing situations that we presented and worked with opened with such statements as:

1. The English people are really creepy — they're so cold and unfriendly. Back in Tallahassee people are nicer to you.
2. I'm homesick. I miss my friends back in Tallahassee and really feel left out here.
3. I really would like to date some Italian (English) girls, but they act like they think American men are all perverts or something. It's really discouraging.
4. Somehow I manage to get left out of everything. I don't know what's wrong.

134 Peer Counseling and Self-help Groups on Campus

At the end of the first session, the London program trainees had the opportunity to meet with four British subjects, members of the Tallahassee British-American Club. The experience was planned as an opportunity for the trainees to discuss informally the way of life in England and to relate to people from another culture. The discussion included such questions from the trainees as where to meet people, whether the British were as reserved as they were reputed to be, and so forth. Although the session lasted only about an hour and the trainers acted as facilitators, guiding the discussion, the trainees experienced difficulty in relating to the rather formal British manner. Nevertheless it was enlightening for the trainees; the experience and discussion of cultural differences (Pedersen et al., 1976) proved to be more helpful than the factual information conveyed in the meeting. We hope to establish a similar experience for Florence counselors and are currently searching for Italian volunteers.

The second session began, as did all others, with a check for any unfinished business from the previous session. This session we devoted ourselves to an in-depth continuation of dealing with individual interpersonal relations. We began by teaching basic human relations skills, such as paraphrasing, reflecting feelings, and describing one's own feelings. These techniques were described, illustrated, then practiced in one-to-one role playing. Our next teaching session included a presentation of professional issues related to the role of counselor. The critical issues that we stressed included:

1. Level of competence: This issue involves communicating to your client what you are, who you are, and what you do and do not offer in the way of services.
2. Contract of confidentiality: This issue involves keeping confidential information about any one who could be considered a client. It includes appropriate record keeping and how to avoid gossiping.
3. Legal and medical concerns: This issue involves potential liabilities associated with giving unqualified legal or medical advice, and strategies for referring students to legitimate sources of information.

Self-help Training of Student Counselors for Overseas Programs   135

We then went back to our role-playing dyads and presented problems that would give the trainee an opportunity to use both the interpersonal skills and knowledge of the various professional issues presented earlier.

After a break we returned to a group meeting at which trainees could raise questions, share feelings about the progress of training, and bring up any specific problem areas that might need to be dealt with. Following this group meeting we presented a homework assignment, requesting each team to begin developing a rough outline for an orientation program designed to meet anticipated needs of foreign studies students.

In presenting the assignment, we introduced the trainees to the theory of primary prevention. We explained that many of the problems they had seen the previous night could have been prevented or at least mitigated by preventive intervention. For example, homesickness could be helped by the early introduction of activities that could help the student develop new friendships and interests. Just as we had used the "scare wheel" to create motivation for learning counseling skills, we used the stress of role-playing counseling situations to build motivation for learning preventive techniques.

At the beginning of the third session each team of trainees presented its orientation program to the trainers in a role-playing format. To set the scene, we imagined that we were all in the foreign country on the first day after arrival, and that the counselors were presenting their ideas to the student-faculty orientation committee. We responded in roles, giving criticisms as a student or professor might, and thus preparing the trainees for the kinds of negotiation necessary in organizing programs. A trainer in the role of an obsessive administrator might insist that the first hour of the opening orientation session be spent in giving detailed instructions on handling a foreign checking account. The trainees would have to convince the administrator that the students might need more general kinds of information the first night, yet maintain their relationships with him by working out a joint strategy for dealing with his concern in another way. As each team presented its orientation program, we called attention to areas that might be overlooked and attempted to point out practical considerations that they would need to look at in operationalizing their program. In discussing the programs, we stressed that this was not an imaginary exercise, but a trial run of a program they could actually present. We also stressed that if they did not present the programs, no one else would.

In presenting their programs the trainees demonstrated a gratifying amount of group spirit and initiative. They were proud of their work, and had been imaginative in collecting materials. New ideas were presented for programs, such as a get-together at the airport while waiting to board the charter plane. We had attempted to facilitate team cohesion by beginning with individual activities, and then moving toward team activities as the pressure grew more intense from the time constraints, our pressure on the teams, and the effects of fatigue. In attempting to strengthen the teams, we also included in this session a counseling team caucus during which each team met to discuss individual members' strengths and weaknesses, and the kinds of problems each felt comfortable or uncomfortable in handling. The trainers also met to discuss their impressions of the same issues regarding the trainees. We then had a general meeting with trainers and trainees to discuss how, given individual assessments of skills (Tyler et al., 1978), the trainees could best work as a team. For example, a team member might say, "I really don't feel comfortable working with somebody's heavy personal problems, but I enjoy helping to organize trips and other activities." So we found this member's energies focused on programming as one aspect of larger team efforts.

The fourth session was devoted to consultation with administrators and to dealing with group situations. For our first activity we asked the counselors to formulate a statement of skills and expertise of their team that they had worked out at the end of session three. We asked them to develop this statement to present to the Director and his staff, and the faculty, and the students of the foreign studies program. When this was done we had a simulation in which the counselors met with the administrators, played by trainers, to present their team and to work out mutual needs and expectations. We then discussed what had taken place (was the counselor manipulated into doing something he did not want to do, were his own expectations appropriate, did he deal in a helpful, effective way with the administrators?).

Self-help Training of Student Counselors for Overseas Programs   137

Our next training experience was a simulation. The trainers role-played a group of students with various group and individual difficulties at the foreign studies center. The trainees were asked as a team to handle this group of students just as college students (Barrow and Hetherington, 1981) have been shown to lead other groups. We addressed some of the following problems during this group simulation:

1. First, the team as a group had to assess what was going on with these students as a whole.
2. Next, the team had to develop strategies for dealing not only with the whole group problem, but with some of the individual problems as well.
3. The counseling team needed to serve as intermediaries between students and administration.

This simulation has proved very effective for getting the counseling team to rely on its own resources and to use various strategies about interpersonal relations that they have learned. At the end of this role-playing situation, trainers presented their impressions of the impact and effectiveness of the team both as a whole and in the individual situations in which they had performed. Following this we discussed the whole simulation and then moved toward a wrap-up of the entire training program.

Our last activity was working with the trainees to plan and carry out a meeting and social in Tallahassee for students who would be participating in the foreign studies program. This meeting served as the fifth night of the training program. We analyzed the students' needs for information, meeting people, and getting to know the counselors and faculty and worked out strategies for accomplishing these goals. The counselors took charge of the meeting, establishing their roles as leaders and as persons concerned with students, but we were in the background, giving advice when necessary. Thus the beginning counselors were able to practice their large-group leadership skills with consultation before setting out on their own in the foreign setting.

Trainer-Trainee Interaction

One important feature of the trainer-trainee interaction throughout the training program was that whenever possible trainers played various roles, student, director, or whatever, while the trainees played their counselor roles. If the trainees had planned an activity to cheer up the students at a time when morale was low, the trainers would immediately assume their "depressed student" roles, slouch around an imaginary television set, and begin complaining about the weather.

Trainer A: What a cold, drippy place. I wish I was back in Tallahassee.

Trainer B: Yeah, I'm getting sick of it.

Trainee: I hear there's a really interesting exhibit at the Tate. Does anybody want to go?

Trainer B: We've been to about forty museums for art history class. I hope I don't ever see another painting as long as I live.

Trainer A: I've had it with culture. Why can't we have some fun for a change?

Trainee: I've found a really neat Italian restaurant that doesn't cost much. Why don't we all go out to supper and then maybe go to a movie?

Trainer A: I could get into that.

Trainer B: That's a good idea. When do we leave?

Remaining in roles had several advantages. Had the trainers chosen to discuss the relative merits of food versus art as a cure for situational depression in late adolescence, it would have been easy for the trainees to avoid their feelings by intellectualizing at length. Using roles made the interaction more intense, prevented unproductive talking, and allowed the highly intelligent trainees to make their own generalizations from the particular situation to general principles. If the trainees had found themselves hopelessly frustrated, the trainers would have left their roles long enough to make a suggestion or give feedback, and would then have asked the trainees to try again. Even during didactic presentations, impromptu role playing was used to illustrate points as they were being explained. While Trainer A was giving a talk on the ethical considerations involved in giving medical advice, Trainer B broke in with:

Trainer B: Say, Alice, I need some advice. I'm off the pill now and my boyfriend says condoms are just as safe. Is that true?

Trainer C: I have a pamphlet put out by the Planned Parenthood Association that gives statistics on different kinds of contraceptives. Let's look at that and see what they say.

Self-help Training of Student Counselors for Overseas Programs   139

These illustrations helped to clarify the points of the didactic presentations and also to maintain interest by changing the pace of the session.

Though some of the trainers' functions were easily observable, such as role playing and giving feedback, other important responsibilities were far more subtle. One of the trainers' functions was to model with one another the kinds of interaction that we wanted the counselor trainees to develop within their own teams. It was obvious that the trainers liked each other and gave each other a great deal of emotional support during the rather strenuous sessions. The trainers also made it apparent that they were aware of one another's areas of strength and weakness and were able to intensify their impact as a team by letting each person perform the tasks best suited to his unique talents. One trainer was especially tactful and helpful in soothing the anxieties of a trainee who found any criticism painful; another was adept at revitalizing a dragging session with a well-timed joke. The trainers' interactions with the trainees modeled important aspects of the future counselor-student relationship. The trainers demonstrated group leadership skills, ways of giving negative feedback without hurting feelings unnecessarily, and the importance of being sensitive to the feelings of the people with whom they were working.

The trainers' interactions with each other and with the trainees also helped to create an atmosphere of warmth and acceptance that made it easier for the trainees to take risks, try new behaviors, and explore their own ideas and feelings. Trainers made frequent expressions of warmth and concern both toward each other and toward the trainees. In maintaining a supportive atmosphere, it was also important to be very careful about handling negative feedback. We found that most of the trainees, accustomed to the pressures of graduate school, felt a strong need always to be right and found criticism rather frightening. Consequently, we were careful to give feedback in a direct but gentle way and also to model our own willingness to accept criticism and learn from our mistakes. The amount of feedback given during the first night's role playing seemed to have an important effect by letting the trainees know that receiving feedback was not as uncomfortable as they had expected.

140   *Peer Counseling and Self-help Groups on Campus*

The casual style of the meetings, in which everyone sat on the floor in casual clothes also helped reduce the trainees' anxiety. Humor played an important role in relaxing the group, building cohesiveness, and warding off exhaustion. Jokes, kidding, and clowning in roles were common occurrences. There were, however, strong taboos against inappropriate use of humor. It was never used in a way that might make someone feel belittled; for example, negative feedback was always given in a completely serious way. Joking and kidding always were done in a way that called attention to the positive qualities of the person who was the object of a joke.

While the trainers strove to create a supportive atmosphere and to keep tension at a manageable level, they also observed the group carefully for signs of undue tension, fatigue, or other conditions not conducive to training. If a trainer noted that the group was dragging, he might have intervened immediately with a comment such as, "I'm getting tired of talking about ethics. Would anybody else like to do something different for awhile?" Or at one of the frequent trainer conferences during breaks in the program, he might have consulted with other trainers about strategies for energizing the group during the next segment of training. Close attention was also paid to the progress of individual trainees, and plans for individualized attention were made during breaks. A trainers' conference might include a discussion like:

Trainer A: George really freaked out when he had to role-play enforcing the drug rules.

Trainer B: I'm working with him next hour; maybe I'd better throw in some more rule enforcement situations.

Trainer C: From what he was saying at coffee last night, I get the idea that drugs are a really tense subject for him. Maybe you could start off with getting him to enforce something easier and then work up to a drug problem.

This conversation illustrates one of the most important advantages utilizing paraprofessional trainers to ensure a high trainer-trainee ratio. The tasks of keeping track of group and individual dynamics, maintaining a comfortable group atmosphere, and conveying new information to trainees would have been an overwhelming burden to one or two people. With a group of trainers involved

Self-help Training of Student Counselors for Overseas Programs   141

at the same time, one could be observing while another talked; different people tended to focus their attention on different aspects of the total process. Sharing insights with one another gave each trainer a broader perspective than he could have gained from his own observations, and the presence of six to eight trainers ensured that most necessary tasks were done by one person or another.

Implications of the Program

We believe that many aspects of this program could be useful not only for the specific purpose of training overseas program counselors but in other situations (Sue, 1977) in which carefully selected and intelligent but inexperienced people must be trained very quickly to take on roles as helping persons. We found that careful manipulation of group anxiety when coupled with a supportive atmosphere led to a rapid rate of personal exploration and growth. We learned that using role-played simulations or real problems was far more conducive to rapid training than the use of more abstract, descriptive presentations. The use of a sizable number of paraprofessional trainers was an important factor because they made it possible both to give individual attention to each trainee and to model group dynamics (Levy, 1976) in ways similar to other self-help groups. There was also a dual training impact, since the paraprofessional trainers came away from the program with new sophistication in group leadership and program planning.

REFERENCES

Allen, E. E. Paraprofessionals in a large-scale university program. *Personnel and Guidance Journal*, 1974, *53*, 276-280.

Barrow, J., & Hetherington, C. Training paraprofessionals to lead social anxiety management groups. *Journal of College Student Personnel*, 1981, *22*, 269-273.

D'Augelli, A. R., & Danish, S. J. Evaluating training programs for paraprofessionals and nonprofessionals. *Journal of Counseling Psychology*, 1976, *23*(3), 247-253.

Levy, L. H. Self-help groups: Types and psychological processes. *Journal of Applied Behavioral Science*, 1976, *12*(3), 310-322.

Pedersen, P., Lonner, W., & Draguns, J. (Eds.). *Counseling across cultures*. Honolulu: University of Hawaii Press, 1976.

142   *Peer Counseling and Self-help Groups on Campus*

Sue, S. Community mental health services to minority groups: Some optimism, some pessimism. *American Psychologist,* 1977, *32*(8), 616-624.

Sue, S. Training of "third world" students to function as counselors. *Journal of Counseling Psychology,* 1973, *20,* 73-78.

Tyler, M., Kalafat, J. D., Boroto, D. R., & Hartman, J. A brief assessment technique for paraprofessional helpers. *Journal of Community Psychology,* 1978, *6,* 53-59.

Vontress, C. E. Cultural barriers in the counseling relationship. *Personnel and Guidance Journal,* 1969, *48,* 11-17.

Vontress, C. E. Racial differences: Impediments to rapport. *Journal of Counseling Psychology,* 1971, *18,* 7-13.

Chapter 10

STUDENTS AS ADMINISTRATIVE AIDES:
On-the-job Learning

BARBARA A. JACKSON

RESEARCH has indicated that peer helping relationships enjoy a great deal of success, and that when students have conflicts and problems, they often turn to other students even before teachers, family, or professionals (Cohen, 1975; Conroy, 1978; Leventhal et al., 1976). With these findings in mind, the Division of Student Affairs at Florida State University sought to modify student service programs by involving students in the role of administrative paraprofessionals in which they shared the responsibility for service delivery with professional staff. The Vice President for Student Affairs was involving students in all the programs of the division since many of the administrative tasks (DeMoss, 1974) could effectively be done by students. The peer-to-peer involvement was based on the employment of students as members of a professional-paraprofessional administrative team (Oliver and Turner, 1972).

The groundwork was laid in the Fall of 1971 for selecting the paraprofessionals, identifying their roles and functions, and locating the source of funding. The administrative aides were to be selected from among interested undergraduates based on a response to advertisements in the university newspaper. Positions were available in the following six units: Resident Student Development, the University Counseling Center, the University Union and Student Activities, Career Development Service, Minority Student Affairs, and Central Staff of the Divisional office. In each of these units, candidates were interviewed and screened by the director and the professional staff on the basis of creativity and sensitivity to student needs.

Authorization was given for paraprofessional salaries of up to $3.00 an hour and for up to twenty hours of work a week. Actual work time and salaries were left to the discretion of each unit director. Three thousand dollars in support monies, above their salaries, was set aside for the support of special projects.

After the paraprofessionals had been selected, a three-phase orientation and development process was begun as follows: (1) initially each paraprofessional was to spend time in his or her unit becoming thoroughly familiar with its operations; (2) they would then move to the role of an actual staff member; and (3) the students would meet as a group to share experiences and plan group strategies. More specific orientation and training was left to the discretion of each director.

The paraprofessional program actually began in 1972 with seven paraprofessionals (Resident Student Development hired two students by splitting the salary). A month after the program began, both the professional staff and the paraprofessionals felt they needed someone to be in charge of the program. A coordinator was chosen to fill this role and to serve as a liaison between the professional staff and the paraprofessionals. A different group of students was selected for the second year in order to maintain a continual flow of fresh ideas into the program and to make contact with as many students as possible who might be interested in the positions.

The coordinator of the program was by requirement a graduate student, whose duties became more concrete during the second year of the program. Some of her duties included assisting in the selection of paraprofessionals, administering the day-to-day functioning of the program, supervising and providing initial and ongoing training for the paraprofessionals, and providing continuous and final evaluation of the program. This chapter describes the second year of the program.

For the most part, the paraprofessionals worked on an individual basis and attended weekly staff meetings to exchange ideas and report to the coordinator. The coordinator, in turn, served as a consultant to the paraprofessionals and helped them deal with any interpersonal conflicts that arose on the job.

University Counseling Center

It was the responsibility of the University Counseling Center to provide a variety of counseling services to the university community, among them, services specifically for off-campus students. The administrative paraprofessional chose to work in the Office of Off-Campus Counseling at the Counseling Center. Working with its director (Moore, 1974) and preprofessional graduate counseling students, she helped to develop Project Alteract, a nontraditional student drop-in and growth center which sponsored a variety of informal and formal experiences. The paraprofessional was involved in developing the program and organizing activities for the approximately 1200 students who participated in Alteract during the first eighteen months. Working as an administrative aide under the supervision of a professional member of the Counseling Center staff, there were also opportunities to function as a trainer and group leader.

In addition, the paraprofessional aid participated as a voting member in Center staff meetings, wrote quarterly reports, and helped to train student counselors for an overseas study program.

University Student Union Programs and Activities

The University Student Union houses a number of student groups, including student government and the staff of the university student newspaper. It is the central office for student programs and activities, noncredit courses, and leisure activities. The paraprofessional in this unit had to work closely not only with the professional staff, but with student leaders as well.

Administrative activities included the conduct of a student needs assessment with findings and recommendations reported to the student government and planning for the development of a Learning and Resource Center that served as a central computerized clearinghouse of information about housing and roommate selection, curriculum, book exchange programs, and employment opportunities.

146   *Peer Counseling and Self-help Groups on Campus*

Another administrative project involved plans to share the results of faculty course evaluations using the Student Instructional Rating System (S.I.R.S.) with the student body. A letter campaign encouraging various departments to make the results public by way of Faculty Senate decision was initially defeated but ultimately approved.

Resident Student Development

Resident Student Development encompassed not only the student residence halls, but also off-campus apartments for married students and their families, and an off-campus trailer park. The paraprofessional aide was required to live in one of these settings based on the premise that a person would understand and be sensitive to the needs of students with whom he or she shared living facilities.

One of the chief complaints of residence hall students had been their inability to break housing contracts. A student who wished to be released from a contract was required to appear before a Housing Appeals Board to plead his or her case. The paraprofessional aide educated students by explaining the housing appeals procedure and helped to prepare them for their presentations to the board. This effort elicited a wide range of student problems ranging from personal problems with residence hall staff members to problems with the University Health Center and to problems with financial aid. Some of the student concerns were easily handled while others were referred to professional counselors.

Minority Student Affairs

One of the primary jobs of Minority Student Affairs was to meet the needs of international and black students. Many of the international students had difficulty understanding and speaking English. The paraprofessional in this unit established a basic conversational English course for these students through the Center for Participant Education, an arm of the student government that offered nonacademic and noncredit courses such as yoga, candle making, and horseback riding.

She also worked as the hostess for "Reflections on Black," a program broadcast on the university-run television station that attempted to provide greater communication and interaction between the local black community and black university students. In conjunction with black student leaders, she attempted to create new activities on campus for black students designed to alleviate some of the alienation felt by many of them. She also worked very actively with the black student leaders on reorganization of the existing black student union.

Career Development Services

This unit of the Division of Student Affairs functions as a career planning and placement center. It offers students employment information and coordinates a Cooperative Education program in which students may work in their chosen fields and attend school at the same time.

The paraprofessional in this area discovered by means of a survey of the student body that the majority of students were unaware of the services offered by this unit. She decided to devote her time to a publicity campaign on the availability of career-related information.

The campaign included the development of a pamphlet for freshmen and new students describing sources of career information and the services of the Office of Career Planning and Placement. She also worked with the academic departments on campus, urging them to use the Career Development Services as a referral source for students.

She also prepared a tape for the university radio station on helpful hints to assist students with job interviews by illustrating proper and improper responses during a job interview.

Central Staff — Division of Student Affairs

Working as a member of the administrative staff of the Division of Student Affairs, the coordinator of administrative aides assumed a variety of responsibilities including updating the objectives of the program, evaluating the program, writing job descriptions for herself and the other paraprofessionals, and preparing a slide show and script for use in describing the program around the

148   *Peer Counseling and Self-help Groups on Campus*

country, e.g. presentation at conventions such as the National Association of Student Personnel Administrators. The coordinator also prepared documentary program descriptions for use in small group discussions as well as a survey of five paraprofessional programs around the nation.

The general goals of the paraprofessional program included: (1) to maximize information exchange, and to minimize project duplication among paraprofessionals and between paraprofessionals and other unit staff of the Division; (2) to provide opportunities for paraprofessionals to serve as effective liaison between students and the professional staff of the Division; (3) to specify solutions to obstructions that impede student transitions through the University; (4) to assist in the establishment and administration of Divisional duties; and (5) to acquaint paraprofessionals with the complexities associated with the administration of the University and Division of Student Affairs.

The evaluation instrument designed by the coordinator was a self-report device by which the paraprofessionals could evaluate each of the five objectives of the program. It asked the paraprofessionals to assess their efforts in response to a variety of questions, such as identifying the frequency with which they met with individual students.

Selected findings from the evaluation included the following observations by paraprofessional aides: (1) they did not feel that there was any duplication among themselves or between themselves and the professional staff; (2) they met on the average with eight students a week, and several of them met with as many as eight student groups a month; (3) they were available between fifteen and twenty hours per week to speak with students; (4) they were utilized by professional staff in solving problems; (5) they were very active in spotting obstructions to student progress through the university and in specifying remedies to these obstructions; and (6) they assisted in establishing new procedures within their units, and met frequently with unit staff to discuss policy, objectives, and procedures. The paraprofessionals were asked to identify the personal benefits acquired from the program. At the top of the list was "a better understanding of the administration and the hierarchy of the University." They also felt they had grown both personally and professionally as a result of this experience, similar to what Millick et al., (1974) and Brasington (1975) report.

One of the most serious drawbacks of this evaluation is that it does not include the perceptions of the target population served by the paraprofessionals. The overall impact of the program on the consumer was difficult to assess. Some staff observed that the majority of the student body remained unfamiliar with the services of the Division of Student Affairs. Some of the paraprofessional programs ceased after the pilot project period of two years, since students were not using the services that the paraprofessionals provided.

Some of the paraprofessionals felt that they were too much under the thumb of unit directors who would not allow enough freedom or flexibility (Field and Gatewood, 1976) or who provided little support. For some staff, the limited funding to hire a sufficient number of staff was a problem. Several of the paraprofessionals lacked creativity and interpersonal skills, and required close supervision from the professional staff.

Some Guidelines for Future Programs

Several problems emerged during the first two years of the program. For example, student leaders felt the paraprofessionals were "administrative lackies" who could not be trusted and would not serve the interests of students. Many of the complaints appeared to be aimed at the Vice President for Student Affairs who was not on good terms with the student leaders at that time. It is felt this problem could have been handled if the student leaders had been more fully involved at the beginning of the program. Therefore, one guide for future programs is to involve student government leadership early in the development process.

In the first year of the program, the paraprofessionals were paid a good salary, and the program support monies were set aside for their use. The good salaries drew student interest, and there were more applications for the positions the first year than the second. The entire budget the second year of the program was allocated for salaries; the paraprofessionals had no support monies. Their only recourse was to appeal for funds through the directors of their units. The Division began to feel a financial squeeze, and this left the paraprofessionals limited in their capacities to generate projects. It is strongly recommended that future programs include sufficient funds for program development.

A third problem was the selection of the paraprofessionals. Several of the students lacked well-developed interpersonal skills, which became obvious particularly in their dealings with the directors. This is a difficult quality to screen for during the interview process. To improve the selection process, it is recommended that the interviewers and applicants role-play situations in which the students may find themselves. For example, one interviewer might play the role of an irate director, while the student being interviewed responds in the role of paraprofessional. This process should give the interviewers a better idea of the applicant's interpersonal skills.

The paraprofessionals were often frustrated when they could not find enough concerned students to support their projects, or when they had repeated problems in their work. It was difficult for some to integrate themselves into an on-going program. Perhaps this might have been avoided if paraprofessionals with a stronger commitment to the program and a substantial capacity to handle frustration had been hired at the outset. Both academic credit and minimum wage rates might also help to insure the commitment of the students as others (Leventhal et al., 1976) have found.

Much care and caution must be taken in initiating an administrative paraprofessional program. Considerable groundwork must be laid, and enormous energy expended during the initial phase of the program to ensure its success (Conroy, 1978).

REFERENCES

Brasington, J. Thoughts on being a paraprofessional: Some personal notes. Chapter in Schauble, P. G., & Resnick, J. (Eds.), *Paraprofessional counseling: Functions, methods, and issues.* Gainesville: Psychological and Vocational Counseling Center Monograph, Vol. 2, 1975.

Cohen, B. Students counseling students: A personal experience. Chapter in Schauble, P. G., & Resnick, J. (Eds.), *Paraprofessional counseling: Functions, methods, and issues.* Gainesville: Psychological and Vocational Counseling Center Monograph, Vol. 2, 1975.

Students as Administrative Aides: On-the-job Learning

Conroy, J. K. Paid student paraprofessionals. *NASPA Journal*, 1978, *15*(3), 18-24.

DeMoss, R. T. The paraprofessional as administrator: An innovative role. *Personnel and Guidance Journal*, 1974, *53*, 315-318.

Field, H. S., & Gatewood, R. The paraprofessional and the organization: Some problems of mutual adjustment. *Personnel and Guidance Journal*, 1976, *55*(4), 181-185.

Leventhal, A. M., Berman, A. L., McCarthy, B. W., & Wasserman, C. W. Peer counseling on the university campus. *Journal of College Student Personnel*, 1976, *17*, 504-509.

Millick, J. L. et al. Paraprofessionals speak out: What it's all about. *Personnel and Guidance Journal*, 1974, *53*(4), 324-332.

Moore, M. Training professionals to work with paraprofessionals. *Personnel and Guidance Journal*, 1974, *53*(4), 308-312.

Oliver, J., & Turner, N. Students as Administrative Paraprofessionals . . . A Concept for the Future. 1972. Unpublished manuscript. Division of Student Affairs, Florida State University.

Section III
MULTIPLE PERSPECTIVES —
EDUCATIONAL, LEGAL AND
CROSS-CULTURAL

Chapter 11

PARAPROFESSIONALS AND ISSUES OF LEGAL LIABILITY

ERNEST T. BUCHANAN, III

THE last fifteen years has witnessed the emergence of new kinds of counseling (crisis, drug abuse, abortion) performed by new kinds of counselors (peers, self-help and paraprofessionals; law, medical or divinity students) who are located in new kinds of places (outreach centers, storefronts, and telephones). This book illustrates such changes occurring on university campuses.

While university training programs in counselor education, social work, counseling psychology, or clinical psychology prepare graduate students for employment as qualified counseling personnel usually protected by certification or licensing laws, it is important to assess the issues surrounding the legal liability of paraprofessional personnel with limited training.

What is the legal status of the person with less training and experience, such as the peer counselor in the Telephone Counseling Service, the law student, or the paraprofessional in Project Alteract? If such a person functions as a counselor, what standard of performance does the law require? Can the college junior who counsels a client in a university-sponsored peer counseling program be held legally responsible for that client's suicide? Can the director of that counseling center — the professional who supervised the work of the college junior — be held legally responsible for the suicide of that client, on a legal theory of agency? What are the legal responsibilities of the trained professional for the

155

156 *Peer Counseling and Self-help Groups on Campus*

paraprofessional who works under his or her supervision? What are the legal liabilities and responsibilities of the trained counselor, as distinguished from those of the paraprofessional? In order to address some of these questions, it is important to cite critical legal precedents.

Bogust vs. Iverson, 102 N.W. 2d 228 (1960) is the leading case defining the legal responsibility of the trained counselor. Jeannie Bogust was a nineteen-year-old student at Stout State College. In 1957, Ms. Bogust sought the professional counseling assistance of Dr. Iverson, director of the counseling center at Stout State. (Dr. Iverson held the Ph.D. degree.) The counseling center provided the standard services of personal, social and academic testing, assessment and counseling.

Jeannie became Dr. Iverson's client in November, 1957. Iverson administered aptitude and personality tests, and counseled Jeannie until April 15, 1958, when Iverson suggested termination of the counseling relationship. Jeannie committed suicide on May 27, 1958.

At no time during the counseling period did Iverson recommend or attempt to recommend psychiatric care, nor did he advise Jeannie's parents of her state of mind. Jeannie's parents filed suit against Iverson for the wrongful death of their daughter, alleging that Iverson was negligent in that:

1. He was familiar with Jeannie's emotional disturbances, conflicts, and scholastic difficulties.
2. He should have secured psychiatric treatment and advised her parents.

To prove a negligence action, the plaintiff must first prove that Iverson was under a duty to Jeannie to secure psychiatric treatment for her, and to advise her parents of her state of mind.

The trial court held that Iverson was not under a legal duty to Jeannie or her parents, in that Iverson had no training or experience in medical fields that would give him the skills necessary to diagnose mental illness. The appellate court affirmed the trial court, holding that:

1. As a *teacher,* Iverson could not be held to the same degree of care as a person trained in medicine or psychiatry.

2. The duty of advising Jeannie's parents would arise from Iverson's knowledge of a mental emotional state which required medical care.
3. Iverson, as a matter of law, did not know nor could he have reasonably foreseen that Jeannie would take her life.
4. No facts established a causal relationship between Iverson's acts and Jeannie's suicide.

The *Bogust* ruling, then, relieved the Ph.D. counseling center director from any legal duty to seek psychiatric care for a student client on these facts, or to advise the parents of Jeannie's condition. If a trained professional is not found liable on the basis of these facts, this decision indicates that no legal liability would be found against the peer or paraprofessional counselor in a suit based on the *Bogust* facts.

However, one legal writer recently suggested that the *Bogust* decision was "not justified," that a college counselor has a legal duty to take affirmative steps to prevent physical harm to the troubled client (Vanderbilt, 1971). This position was reflected in the case of *McBride vs. State,* 227 N.Y.S. 2d 80 (1967), 294 N.Y.S. 2d 265 (1968). In *McBride,* a fifteen-year-old student in a state residential training school was corporally disciplined by a residential counselor for exposing himself to a female attendant. The residential counselor was forbidden the use of the corporal punishment. The student committed suicide subsequent to being disciplined. The parents of the child who had committed suicide sued the state of New York to recover for the wrongful death of the child. The court found liability, holding the school to the same standard of care as a private enterprise, ruling that the extensive control over the student obliged the school to know the state of mind of a fifteen-year-old child, and to exercise a reasonable degree of care to protect the child from injury, "self-inflicted or otherwise."

McBride and *Bogust* obviously differ in several aspects. First, the age of the students was different. As defined by today's laws, Ms. Bogust was an adult, the McBride boy a child. One's responsibilities to a child are obviously greater than to an adult. Second, the setting and degree of control in the two cases was distinctly different. A state residential training facility for troubled youngsters is quite different from the walk-in counseling service provided by a state university. Third, the state of the law in 1967 and in 1960 was quite different with regard to schools and colleges. In 1960, a suit against a college was a rare event. In 1967, suits against colleges had become fairly numerous. Fourth, the defendant in *McBride* violated a specific rule forbidding corporal punishment, a rule that established the minimal legal duty of care, while no similar rule, practice or policy could be cited in *Iverson* as establishing a legal duty. Fifth, in *McBride* the suicide occurred within hours after the discipline, while weeks elapsed from the termination of Jeannie's interviews till the date of her suicide. Finally, the physical assault in *McBride* can be sharply distinguished from the mere termination of a counseling relationship in *Bogust*.

Several conclusions may be drawn from the *Bogust* and *McBride* cases. When an institution presents itself to the public as exercising a custodial training function, employees of that institution, whether the institution is public or private, may be held to the "reasonable man" standard against which negligence is measured. This means that paraprofessionals employed in residential facilities may be subject to personal liability, or may, by their actions, subject the supervisor or the institution to liability. Such liability may be found more easily where a paraprofessional fails to follow procedures governing the operation of such a center. Where services are offered in a noncustodial setting, strict compliance with reasonable operating procedures remains important.

Despite the apparent limitation on the liability of the trained counselor set forth in *Bogust* (and hence, presumably, for the paraprofessional as well), it is important that the supervisor of paraprofessionals note that ignorance or the disregard of procedures by paraprofessionals may not provide much legal defense. Prosser states that:

> The reasonable man may be found negligent when he proceeds, conscious of his own ignorance, into a situation in which he causes danger to others. The special relationship between a school and its students is sufficient to place a heavy burden on the school to determine its own ignorance (Prosser, 1973).

An examination of the general law governing the liability of the counselor for a suicide reminds us of the special burden placed on those in a helping relationship. Suicide is defined as a deliberate intentional act by an individual. While, by tradition, few courts will establish civil liability for causing suicide, the numerical increase in the suicide rate has led to an increasing number of tort suits. Several jurisdictions are now permitting recovery of damages in suicide cases.

Under the current law, an individual who intentionally brings about a suicide or lesser emotional harm can be found liable. In addition, tort law has imposed an affirmative duty of care on individuals in helping roles. The reasonable man who proceeds to provide counseling which causes harm when the counselor is or ought to be "conscious of his own ignorance" may be deemed liable.

This liability imposes a heavy duty on professional staff providing leadership for outreach, residential, or other facilities manned primarily by volunteers. Volunteers must be carefully selected, trained, supervised and evaluated. Under the *McBride* decision, supervision of volunteers in residential settings is especially important.

In the absence of a privileged relationship, a qualified counselor called to testify should investigate the possibility of asserting one of the following:

a. The Psychologist-Patient Relationship. A school or other counselor licensed as a psychologist can, in the seventeen states where such a privilege is established, assert this privilege.

b. Assertion of Hearsay Rule. Generally a witness may not testify to that which he heard another say. However, there are many exceptions to the hearsay rule, including the party-admission exception, the dying declaration exception, and the declaration against interest exception.

c. Judicially Extended Privilege. The counselor may ask the judge that he not be compelled to testify.

d. Ethical Standards. The counselor may ask the court to recognize the ethical standard of the counseling profession.

e. Perjury. The Counselor can always perjure himself/herself, either by saying the client said nothing, or by testifying falsely about the conversation.

f. Silence. The counselor can refuse to answer questions, possibly subjecting himself/herself to a contempt citation.

The status of one type of counselor is illustrative of the situation of the "new" professional or paraprofessional in regard to privileged relationships (California, 1973). Mental illness ranks with heart disease and cancer as one of the nation's greatest health problems. There simply are not enough professional mental health workers to serve the needs of our communities, especially our poorer communities.

To summarize, liability increasingly may be found for damage caused by a counselor or the paraprofessional. The state of the law currently provides little support for a confidential relationship between the counselor, whether trained or paraprofessional, and the client. The greater legal burden is placed on the professional who supervises the work of the paraprofessional. The professional should select, train, supervise, and evaluate volunteers carefully and should carry liability insurance for themselves and their volunteers.

REFERENCES

Bogust vs. Iverson, 10 Wis. 129, 102 N.W. 2d 288 (1960).

"Civil Liability for Causing Suicide," 24 Vanderbilt Law Review 217 (March, 1971).

Comment, "Underprivileged Relations," 61 California Law Review 1050 (1973).

In Re: Grand Jury Subpoena by Gordon Verplanck, 329 F. Supp. 433 (C. D. Cal. 1971).

McBride vs. State, 277 N.Y.S. 2d 80 (1967), 294 N.Y.S. 2d 265 (1969).

"Parental Right to Inspect School Records," 20 Buffalo L.R. 255 (Fall, 1970).

"Privileged Communication Between Participants in Group Psychotherapy," Journal of Law and Social Order 191 (1970).

Prosser, *Law of Torts*, West Publishing Company, Section 32 at 163, 1973.

"Testimonial Privileges . . . ," 56 Iowa Law Review 1323 (1971).

Chapter 12

PEER COUNSELING VIEWED
FROM A CROSS-CULTURAL PERSPECTIVE

JULIAN WOHL

STUDENTS in universities in Asia have difficulties just as their counterparts do in other parts of the world. The range is not unusual; it includes ordinary, developmental problems as well as unique or emotionally severe problems. Counseling and guidance in a systematic, professional sense is, however, a relatively new addition to the Asian scene and peer counseling like that in this country is not yet fully accepted (Powers, 1977). Possibilities for using students as peer helpers in the universities of Asia do exist, and there are important considerations for professionals (Betz, 1980; Wagenfeld and Robin, 1981), students, and educators.

The use of students to help students is clearly now a movement of its own, having succeeded in gaining respectability and acceptance within the professional student services community (Delworth, Sherwood, and Casaburri, 1974; Zimpfer, 1974). This adaptive response, however, is possible because student services can be understood by the larger society. This is not the case on the campuses of Asian universities. Externally imposed requirements and pressures control professions to a far greater degree in Asia than in the United States.

Asian societies view their universities and student services from perspectives significantly different from those in the United States.

The differences relate to the historical function and the contemporary roles of Asian universities and to specific Asian socio-cultural characteristics and traditions. Except Japan, Asian nations are considered generally to be "developing" countries.

Population growth places increasing pressure on education at all levels. The number of students has grown faster than education is able to grow to absorb them; and there is a shortage of good teachers and a need for student advising as noted in Bonar's paper here. Unemployment is high and increasing and these countries are primarily producers of raw materials rather than of manufactured goods. There are serious shortages of the managerial, technical and professional skills needed to promote industrial development. Illiteracy remains a serious problem throughout the area; intra-societal linguistic divisions are often deep and there are powerful, ethnic and cultural, intra-nation group conflicts.

Gunnar Myrdal (1968) says modernization and development, usually thought of in economic terms, have their psychological concomitants: as a society commits itself to industrialization, and virtually all of Asia has, change must occur also in the character of its people. If student personnel services are to flourish in Asian educational settings, their objectives must relate to national development objectives, as well as the needs for psychological support and change.

Higher education in Asia originated from the European requirement to develop a small, home-grown bureaucracy to perform clerical and administrative roles in the colonial areas. The institutions that developed in the nineteenth and early twentieth century were European in concept. This model was also highly congruent with the traditional Asian attitude that the educated person performs no manual labor beyond that involved in manipulating a pen and moving papers (Myrdal, 1968; Fisher, 1964; DuBois, 1973).

During the thirty years after World War II universities were looked upon as critical agents in the national development process (Fisher, 1965; Smith and Carpenter, 1974; Myrdal, 1968). They were to be the producers of knowledge and human resources needed in the effort toward modernization. This effort is unfinished and there are still unresolved problems, including: (1)

Peer Counseling Viewed from a Cross-cultural Perspective   163

shifting conceptions of university education from traditional Asian models of learning; (2) insufficient attention to student learning motivations and attitudes; (3) responding to the vast changes that university education imposes upon the student's life patterns; and (4) matching the skills needed by the society with the traditional academic offerings.

Students and Their Problems

Student personnel services, as an integral part of the university community were not included in the European tradition which served as a model for most universities in the region. Neither was there anything in the Asian tradition that would inject any special concern for the student-as-a-person as the basis for the development of a supportive student personnel structure. Academic advising programs are not generally available on Asian campuses. Faculties are small in relation to large student enrollments, teaching loads are heavy, and salaries are so low that some faculty must find second jobs. There is little time or incentive for faculty to deal with students outside of class. There is nothing in the tradition of the faculty or the administration to generate any special interest in a guidance function.

Nevertheless, in the past twenty years or so a small but occasionally vigorous professional guidance and counseling movement has emerged in Asia. Training programs are limited and few, and most are oriented toward secondary school counseling. Guidance and testing office signs are visible on campuses, but are usually inadequately staffed.

Asian students entering university life are often shocked by the differences between large communal living facilities and their familiar and small family homes. From a structured, family dominated life, they enter an open communal living situation in which the only responsibility is to their classes and academic performance. Their previous education and the atmosphere of the university teaches them to worry about examinations and obtaining a degree, but not about any other aspects of their personal and social development. There is little perception of the need to settle upon a regular, disciplined academic working life. Their conception of the university is apt to be of a rung in the ladder leading

164   *Peer Counseling and Self-help Groups on Campus*

to the social security of a government job, equating education with a degree and its achievement with a career and status (Fisher, 1963, 1964, 1965; Silverstein and Wohl, 1964, Smith and Carpenter, 1974).

In most of the region, traditional values restrict the young person's exploration of heterosexual social relations before college. Freedom from the immediate familiar and local reminders of these constraints, and the secularization of values in the urban university communities, promotes increased sexual consciousness and conflicts. The pressures are heightened in the less structured living conditions, yet the sexes have little preparation for interacting (Fisher, 1964).

Those who are motivated toward learning and personal intellectual growth face the fact that little, either in their previous education or in the university, prepares them to proceed. Their tradition required a passive memorization of specified material to prepare for examinations, and the university continues the pattern. Yet, somehow, they must develop knowledge that university education is an active process in which critical judgment needs to be developed and independent reading beyond the prescribed syllabus needs to be pursued. A major hindrance to the adoption of independent and analytic thinking is the tradition of giving unquestioning respect and deference to the authority of the teacher and the parents (Wilson, 1972; DuBois, 1973). In most Asian societies, the hierarchy of status is clear and the subordinate does not openly disagree with or criticize the superior. It is noteworthy that where Asian self-help and nonprofessionalism have already made inroads, such as medical practice in China, the nonprofessional is accorded more authority and respect than in the United States or Western Europe (Sidel, 1976; Goplerud, 1977).

Peer Intervention Possibilities

The most obvious and easiest introduction of peer counseling on Asian campuses could be in orientation programs initiated prior to and continuing on during the early days of a freshman's campus life. Trained upperclassmen could be assigned to manageably sized groups as guides, first to the physical campus and then

Peer Counseling Viewed from a Cross-cultural Perspective   165

to its social and academic features. Regular meetings might be held in which information about campus organization and living, prepared in advance by the professionals and the peers, could be presented and discussed in structured but informal meetings. Dormitory advisors should be trained to respond positively to the questions of students who should be encouraged to approach them as necessary.

As time passes the orientation sessions would lose some of their emphasis upon entry problems, and the discussions could shift to consideration of the purposes of being in a university as well as attitudes and practices about the learning process. The main service the peer counselor could perform here is to open up the question for discussion so that students could consider or reconsider career choices, but most of all, they should realize that the question is one that they have a right, a privilege, and even an obligation to consider. The questions might be self-directed of their own natures, talents, and abilities, as well as directed to the realities of various career possibilities. An important side-effect of peer counseling might be to serve as a communication bridge between the student and a professional counselor. If peer counseling is successful, there will be a need for referral resources for the professional. This would serve the dual function of getting help to students who would not themselves approach the professional, and by introducing the professionals to more members of the student body, strengthening the position of guidance and counseling on the campus.

In summary, this brief discussion cannot do justice to the continually widening possibilities for the use of students to help other students (Levin, 1976). Different student problems and concerns require unique programmatic responses. It would be unwise to design a program that did not include a careful assessment of the cultural system in which intervention is to occur.

A major problem, perhaps *the* major problem in developing peer counseling in Asia, is the shortage of qualified professionals to help develop the program and to select, train and supervise the peer counselors. Given the lack of services for students, however, one might argue that peer counseling is the least costly method to begin the development of student services. In that way, one or

166   *Peer Counseling and Self-help Groups on Campus*

two professionals could quickly have a substantial impact upon a large university community. Collaborative efforts between Asians and foreign professionals are needed to support the development of student services programs in Asian universities and thereby increase the number of trained Asian professionals.

REFERENCES

Betz, E. The counselor role. Chapter 7 in Delworth, U., & Hanson, G. R. (Eds.), *Student services: A handbook for the profession.* San Francisco: Jossey-Bass, 1980.

Delworth, U., Sherwood, G., & Casaburri, N. *Student paraprofessionals: A working model for higher education.* Student Personnel Series No. 17. Washington: APGA Press, 1974.

DuBois, C. Schooling, youth and modernization in Inda. In Wiggins, W. H., & Guyot, J. F. (Eds.), *Population, politics and the future of Southern Asia.* New York: Columbia University Press, 1973.

Fisher, J. The university student in South and South-East Asia. *Minerva,* Autumn, 1963, 39-53.

Fisher, J. *Universities in Southeast Asia.* International Education Monograph No. 6. Columbus: Ohio State University Press, 1964.

Fisher, J. Education and political modernization in Burma and Indonesia. *Comparative Educational Review,* 1965, *9*(3), 282-287.

Goplerud, E. Mental health systems in the People's Republic of China. Unpublished Ph.D. qualifying paper, State University of New York at Buffalo, 1977. (Available from E. Goplerud, Department of Psychology, 4230 Ridge Lea, Buffalo, N.Y.)

Levin, L. S. Self-care: An international perspective. *Social Policy,* 1976, *7*(2), 70-75.

Myrdal, G. *Asian drama.* Vol. III. New York: Pantheon, 1968.

Powers, W. L. Guidance and counseling in the Far East. Chapter in Drapela, V. J. (Ed.), *Guidance in other countries.* Tampa: University of South Florida, 1977.

Sidel, R. V. Self-help and mutual aid in the People's Republic of China. Chapter 21 in Katz, A. H., & Bender, E. I. (Eds.), *The strength in us.* New York: Franklin Watts, 1976.

Silverstein, J., & Wohl, J. University students and politics in Burma. *Pacific Affairs,* 1965, *37*(1), 50-65.

Smith, T. M. & Carpenter, H. F. Indonesian university students and their career aspirations. *Asian Survey,* 1974, XIV (Sept., No. 9), 807-826.

Wagenfeld, M. O., & Robin, S. S. Reality, rhetoric and the paraprofessional: A concluding note. Section 4 in Robin, S. S., & Wagenfeld, M. O. (Eds.), *Paraprofessionals in the human services.* New York: Human Sciences Press, 1981.

Wilson, D. *Asia awakes.* Middlesex, England: Penguin, 1972.

Zimpfer, D. G. (Ed.). *Paraprofessionals in counseling, guidance and personnel services.* APGA Reprint Series No. 5. Washington: APGA Press, 1974.

Chapter 13

CAN EXPERIENTIAL PROGRAMS
HELP THE LIBERAL ARTS?

HAROLD A. KORN

EXPERIENTIAL education as exemplified in the training and activities of college student peer counseling or self-help programs provokes controversy. It departs from conventional didactic teaching and learning, makes us face value dilemmas in higher education. Experiential programs that combine work, study and volunteerism allow students to test out what is being learned, test out themselves and their motivation, all components of a broadened view of higher education (Sanford, 1964; Katz, 1968). Yet there is continued suspicion among some faculty about the value of experiential education, leading us to consider where the newer efforts (Rodgers and Widick, 1980; Drum, 1980; Brown, 1980) fit in, why they have received a mixed reception and the psychology of their appeal and function.

Higher education's mishaps can be seen if we begin by recalling Daniel Bell's (1968) cogent statement about the objectives of undergraduate education:

> The distinctive function of the college must be to teach modes of conceptualization, explanation and verification of knowledge. As between the secondary school, with its emphasis on primary skills and factual data and the graduate or professional school, whose necessary concern is with specialization and technique, the distinctive function of the college is to deal with the grounds of knowledge: not what one knows but how one knows. The college can be the unique place where students acquire self-consciousness, historical consciousness and methodological consciousness.

Can Experiential Programs Help the Liberal Arts? 169

> ... All knowledge is liberal (that is, enlarges and liberates the mind) when it is committed to continuing inquiry (p. 8).

Most individuals employed in the enterprise of higher education would agree about the importance of the objective of intellectual growth. Yet the day-to-day experience of the approximately 8 million students enrolled in college would reveal plentiful discrepancies and contradictions of this objective (Feldman and Newcomb, 1969). We would find students being exposed to the predigested content of highly specialized disciplines in an array of courses that are conceived of as independent units of instruction. There is even evidence that the existing undergraduate curriculum is an inappropriate educational experience for the nearly 50 percent of the student body who drop out (Cope, 1978).

Higher education shares the larger society's ambivalence about promoting personal freedom and intellectual development for each individual. The poignancy of this ambivalence is reflected in the discrepancy between Bell's beautifully articulated quote on the philosophy of a liberal education and the current status of the undergraduate curriculum due to the faculty reward structure in universities. Faculty success depends on scholarly productivity and it, in turn, is largely dependent on a commitment to specialized knowledge.

Undergraduate curricula provide primitive tools for the transition from youth to adulthood, so we have aborted Bell's "continuing inquiry." Our society focuses on the physical conquest of the environment, success as defined by consumption of natural resources, and escape from the existential conditions of human vulnerability (Illich, 1973). Scientific research, generally basic research, has become the most prestigious activity within the university, with the inquiry framed by the structure of knowledge in a given discipline. Faced with a reward structure that has emphasized research and graduate training, academic administrators have avoided the educational needs of the millions of new undergraduates. Students can "learn" the content of the liberal art's curriculum, yet be unable to demonstrate any personal sequelae of this "mastery" in their own lives.

Intellectual Development

An important source of confusion stems from the failure to distinguish between "learning" and "intellectual development."

170 *Peer Counseling and Self-help Groups on Campus*

Piaget suggests that intelligence is a special instance of adaptation, since life is a continuous creative interaction between the organism and the environment (Hunt, 1961). If one perceives or understands something new in terms of an already existing cognitive structure it is called "assimilation." For example, when a student learns from a textbook about the executive and legislative functions of state government after understanding such functions at the level of the Federal government, much of this learning would be assimilative.

The process of "accommodation" describes what can happen when an individual is confronted with a problem that cannot be understood or solved within his or her existing cognitive structure. Our government student, if now an intern, might quickly be faced with a host of questions about the actual functioning of government that were not even hinted at in the textbook. Were the intern motivated to understand and inquire about this level of government functioning, new concepts would have to be added to his or her cognitive structure.

Both assimilation and accommodation are essential to survival during the early years of adapting to a complex environment. Language usage is embedded in action, and perception is largely determined by the situation (for children); but as intellectual development matures, the individual is able to free thought from the constraints of the moment. Bruner (1972, p. 5) suggests that "Man gradually acquires the means of being able easily to talk of the absent, the possible, the interesting, the unfulfilled, the conditional, the false." This capacity brings with it the potential to rely upon assimilative processes to solve new problems and acquire new learning. Multiple choice tests and even the ubiquitous "compare and contrast" essay examination do not create sufficient conditions for accommodation to take place.

Experiential Education and Accommodation

Experience-based educational programs have the potential to challenge the student in such a way (Mosher and Sprinthall, 1971) that old learning patterns are insufficient and accommodation is required. Such potential can be understood in terms of the number of experiential modalities or the number of sources of information with which the student is required to cope. Students here are given more responsibility for learning or changing. They learn from and teach each other, and such programs are often individualized by differing approaches. Group discussions and didactic techniques are frequent, but so are varied formats, such as video, role-play, and communications exercises (Carkhuff, 1969).

Traditional, discipline-oriented educational programs severely restrict the number of modalities or information channels they use to promote and evaluate learning. The modality given almost exclusive attention is grammatical, oral and written language. Verbal facility permits many new linguistically-based experiences to be handled in terms of previously learned verbal patterns, so new challenges are often coped with by assimilation.

By contrast, experience-based programs offer multiple channels of experience to enhance growth and learning. They confront the student with problem situations that require something in addition to the use of language-based reasoning. When the student is required to act or focus on the total impact of an experience, these varied channels of human communication become activated to serve as sources of information available to the student. Images, feelings, sensations, and fantasies contribute such a universe of discourse.

Great literature, a key element in any liberal arts curriculum, has long been recognized as having potential for promoting intellectual and personal growth. Students can be exposed to these courses and perform quite well, yet experience little personal or intellectual growth. The traditional academic approach provides the student with a set of analytic tools but does not require that he or she relate self-understanding to the understanding of a particular character. The single biggest failure of this traditional approach is that it does not provide the basis for Bell's "continued inquiry."

For accommodation or intellectual growth to take place, on the other hand, the student must experience a question or dilemma. The usual way of understanding, assimilation, must temporarily fail in a way that leaves the individual feeling challenged. When our previous modes of adapting fail us, we usually find a way of escaping the questions or the dilemma. It is just at this point that experiential learning can play a crucial role; as literature is tied to the individual's pursuit of self-understanding, previously untapped sources of motivation become available. Students can also be required to examine themselves in the light of their personal reactions to the characters. How are their personalities similar or different? How would they react under similar circumstances? How are their past learning histories similar to or different from those of the characters? What new feelings or thoughts do they have about themselves as they respond to the literary work? This approach brings the domain of established culture — literature — into direct contact with the student's personal frame of reference.

Another step is required to promote what Bell calls "methodological consciousness." Here it would be essential to involve the student in a critical examination of the novelist's frame of reference — the social and personal factors that influenced the creation of the writing.

The legislative internship mentioned earlier will provide the real life drama and complexity also to engage other students in the accommodative process. The transition from expanded self-awareness to methodological consciousness is also present in this example. The day-to-day politics of the legislative process would undoubtedly engage some students in a self-reflective process, but the next step would engage the student in some aspect of critical inquiry related to man's effort and need to govern.

The enormous popularity of experience-based programs in self-help and peer assistance is the result of starting with the student's frame of reference. The suspicion created by this approach in the minds of some faculty is that the orientation is anti-intellectual and does not belong in the university. The discipline orientation and the experiential orientation each promote only a part of genuine inquiry, and marriage between them seems necessary. But the typical professor and the typical helping professional do not feel they want to be related, even by marriage. What is needed are new programs that work, so that everyone may claim a rightful part in the heritage! We have mounting social action or service needs that students with experiential educational

Can Experiential Programs Help the Liberal Arts? 173

backgrounds are better equipped to meet (Austin and Mahoney, 1967). As we move toward a more service-oriented society, college students with peer or self-help experiences develop the requisite skills for the professions and community leadership.

REFERENCES

Austin, M. J., & Mahoney, S. C. The helping arts: An expanded definition of the social sciences. *New Perspectives: The Berkeley Journal on Social Welfare*, 1967, *1*(2), 45-52.

Bell, D. *The reforming of general education.* Garden City, New York: Doubleday Anchor Books, 1968.

Brown, R. D. The student development educator role. Chapter 8 in Delworth, U., & Hanson, G. R. (Eds.), *Student services: A handbook for the profession.* San Francisco: Jossey-Bass, 1980.

Bruner, J. *The uses of immaturity in social change and human behavior.* (DHEW Pub. No. (HSM) 72-9122, 1972).

Carkhuff, R. R. *Helping and human relations.* New York: Holt, Rinehart & Winston, 1969.

Cope, R. G. Why students stay, why they leave. Chapter in Noel, L. (Ed.), *Reducing the dropout rate: New directions for student services.* (Number 3). San Francisco: Jossey-Bass, 1978.

Drum, D. Understanding student development. Chapter 2 in Morrill, W. H., & Hurst, J. C. (Eds.), *Dimensions of intervention for student development.* New York: John Wiley & Sons, 1980.

Feldman, K. A., & Newcomb, T. M. *The impact of college.* San Francisco: Jossey-Bass, 1969.

Hunt, J. McV. *Intelligence and experience.* New York: Ronald Press, 1961.

Illich, I. *Tools for conviviality.* New York: Perennial Library, Harper & Row, 1973.

Katz, J. (Ed.), *No time for youth.* San Francisco: Jossey-Bass, 1968.

Mosher, R. L., & Sprinthall, N. A. Psychology education: A means to promote personal development during adolescence. *Counseling Psychology,* 1971, *2*, 3-82.

Rodgers, R. F., & Widick, C. Theory to practice: Uniting concepts, logic, and creativity. Chapter 1 in Newton, F. B., & Ender, K. L. (Eds.), *Student development practices.* Springfield, Ill.: Charles C Thomas, Publisher, 1980.

Sanford, N. (Ed.), *College and character.* New York: John Wiley & Sons, 1964.

EPILOGUE:
Implications for the Future

IT is important to take stock of what has been learned so that we may institutionalize our successes and avoid past mistakes from more than a decade of experience with peer support through counseling and self-help strategies. Such an analysis needs to take into account the perspectives of administrators, mental health professionals, paraprofessional student counselors, and students as service recipients. These perspectives will be addressed by identifying key organizational issues, defining need and program philosophy, specifying administrative viewpoints, highlighting student paraprofessional issues, and citing the central program evaluation dilemmas. The basic issues include gaining administrative financial support, organizational legitimation, generic vs. specialized student training, and the complexities of selecting student paraprofessionals (Brown & Delworth, 1977; Ender & McFadden, 1980).

Overview of Key Issues

One of the most complex issues confronting campus peer support programs is gaining and sustaining *administrative support* from university administrators. Key decision-makers are under constant pressure to get the "biggest bang for the buck" from student services funds and must continuously advocate for such scarce funding in competition with requests for instructional or research funds. Competition for limited resources means that student services must demonstrate their value and contribution to the basic educational, human development, and research mission of most colleges and universities.

Epilogue: Implications for the Future

Student service programs need commitment and help from the university beyond financial resources. The organizational location of a peer counseling program, for example, within the hierarchy of university administration can spell success or failure. Possible organizational locations include the Office of the Vice President of Student Affairs, the Director of Student Health or Mental Health Services, the Director of Residence Facilities, the Office of Admissions and Registration, or the Office of Internships and Special Programs. Some will argue that organizational support must emanate from the highest administrative offices while others suggest that decentralized peer counseling and self-help programs are more successfully supported in organizational units directly related to specialized services, e.g. residence halls, advising offices, health and mental health services, etc. Similarly, the access to other campus resources such as space, staff support, materials, and money will be determined, in part, by the location of peer counseling and self-help programs. While administrative support will vary as a function of the organizational history, student needs, and politics of any given campus, it is clear that program stability is closely related to organizational location.

Another major issue is the *training* of student paraprofessionals. Some argue for generic helping skills training while others identify the need for specialized training in such areas as educational advising, community organizing, group leadership, and information and referral. In addition to the training goals or objectives, the length of training and the competence of the trainer are important issues. If training is too long, it is likely to resemble pre-professional or Associate of Arts degree programs and be viewed as competitive and redundant. If it is too short, students may feel that they are ill-equipped to serve clients who may withdraw from or complain about the services. Similarly, if the training program itself is not managed and delivered by competent staff, the student paraprofessionals will not be prepared to deliver effective services and thereby may resign from their volunteer status. Even the concept of volunteering is coming under increasing attack as students need to find salaried experiences to support themselves in an environment of steadily rising educational costs. Some students will continue to be satisfied by earning

176   *Peer Counseling and Self-help Groups on Campus*

college credit while others will recognize the value of free training and the volunteer experience to their personal and career development.

The selection of student paraprofessionals partly (some say largely) determines the nature of training and program success. In order to select only the most qualified and competent students for sensitive counseling and organizing positions, it may be necessary to move beyond the limitations of tests and questionnaires, even screening interviews, to a candid evaluation of student performance as a trainee. This costly and controversial approach may prove to be an important step in increasing the credibility of peer counseling services as well as a mechanism for quality control. Such a process is very time consuming if it is necessary to train twenty students in order to select ten strong performers. Alternative levels and types of peer positions may help handle those students who were not selected for counseling positions. Yet the successful completion of training is only the first step, since ongoing supervision and successful job performance are required if high quality services are to be maintained. Without high quality services, there can be very little administrative, faculty, or student support. The complex process of student selection, training, deployment, evaluation, and additional in-service training represents another one of the key issues in the management of peer counseling and self-help programs.

Defining Need and Program Philosophy

How does one define the need for peer counseling and self-help services? Professional experience and theoretical bias help dictate staff recommendations. The observations of mental health professionals who counsel students primarily during states of crisis, for instance, produce profound implications for program development. For such clinical staff with strong psychopathology orientations may seek peer counselors to help manage the demand for services, at least to serve those in less disturbed condition. Human services staff, however, who may have a strong ecological systems orientation will want student self-help organizers to address the environmental and group life antecedents of isolation, alienation, and role confusion during stressful transitions.

Epilogue: Implications for the Future

Assessing "needs" in contrast to "wants" is always a difficult process. Is there really a need for a new student service? If students are aware of services, will they actually use them rather than relying on friends? Are new services simply the brainchild of professionals who see peer counselors as an easy and inexpensive means for experimenting with new service delivery ideas? Or are student paraprofessionals recruited to solve personnel problems inherent in expanding an existing counseling service? The academic advising process is a good case in point as it has been a source of chronic student frustration at most schools for years. The majority of faculty members on most campuses are ill-equipped to advise students except in their own specialty area; and even here, listening actively, planning careers, providing accurate, timely information and referral are rarely carried out skillfully or effectively. While the need for educational advising is critical, it is not always clear how such needs should be translated into programmatic responses. One solution might involve training faculty, providing both workload credit and tangible rewards for these vital educational services. Another solution, of course, is to train students to carry out this function, even though this violates Wagenfeld & Robin's (1981) warning that peer programs steer clear of areas where professional (faculty) claims are strong. But student-managed educational advising programs usually are not recognized by faculty as of comparable value to their own advising; witness the typically infrequent referrals from faculty or the dubious campus public opinion about such advising services.

Standard needs assessment techniques can be used on campus as well as the community. These include (1) interviewing key student and faculty leaders, (2) conducting an open forum or town hall meeting to identify needs, (3) random sample survey questionnaires to students and faculty, (4) use of existing demographic data on the student body related to age, sex, race, home town, etc., and (5) use of existing records related to student performance to identify the academic needs of students (Warheit et al., 1977).

The documentation and dissemination of current programmatic responses to student needs is also necessary. The guiding philosophy of a particular peer counseling or self-help program must be clearly articulated to staff, participants, and the campus community. Such a philosophy (Alley et al., 1979) serves as a foundation for staff communication and training, for program planning, and for the maintenance of staff morale and a positive political climate for the program on campus. Staff leadership is also a prerequisite to the effective documentation and dissemination of a guiding program philosophy. Generic administrative skills such as planning, organizing, staffing, directing, coordinating, reporting, budgeting, and evaluating should make it possible to document the program impact on service providers and service recipients. For example, it has been observed (Gershon & Biller, 1977) that student paraprofessionals experience the following: (1) increased sense of competence, (2) opportunities to explore career options, (3) acquire experience relevant to graduate education, (4) increased confidence and self-worth, (5) job-satisfaction, (6) increased range of personal contacts on and off campus, and (7) the tangible benefits of course credit and/or monetary remuneration. These observations require more rigorous documentation through evaluative research and must be matched by corresponding inquiries into the impact of peer counseling and self-help programs upon the recipients and participants.

Administrative Perspectives

The identification and selection of natural helpers and student organizers for paraprofessional roles is a complicated administrative issue. Such a personnel management process involves the search for "therapeutic personalities," students with the experience and temperament to be effective peer counselors, and for the "natural organizers," students with sufficient group experience and orientation to change. Considerable administrative skill is required to identify, encourage, screen, train, and evaluate such student paraprofessionals. Once such students are deployed in different programs, it is also necessary to assist all professional as well as paraprofessional staff in recognizing the value and responsibility inherent in participatory management. Student paraprofessionals need to be involved in all levels of decision making if their contribution is to be recognized and utilized. This involvement

Epilogue: Implications for the Future   179

troubles those professionals who view students as transient staff members who are naive in the ways of organizational life, just as some professionals in the community (Pearl, 1974) have avoided a full commitment to paraprofessionals. Equally important is the process of involving students in other aspects of the student affairs organization, programs different from their own, in order to provide a systems perspective on the relationship of their program to other segments of the organization. All staff, including students, need to be oriented to the complexities and the interrelatedness of organizational life in order to function effectively on the job (Delworth, 1974).

Another personnel management issue relates to the use of job descriptions. All staff need to see a written expression of organizational expectations, so that the job description may orient students both to their authority and responsibility. Job descriptions should not be treated as routine bureaucratic documents, but rather as evolving statements that emerge from the resources of the program assigned to meet the needs of service recipients. Since they represent a mutually agreed-upon contract between the supervisor and the peer counselor or self-help organizer, the job descriptions should be useful, referred to regularly, and updated as circumstances change. In addition, job descriptions need to be related to one another so that students can see how the program goals and objectives are translated into specific yet coordinated staff duties and responsibilities. The interrelatedness of job descriptions also provides an opportunity to develop student career ladders so that one might progress from a position of peer counselor trainee, to counselor, to senior counselor, to supervisor of peer counselors. Such a progression helps to signify the organization's commitment to staff advancement and growth, even for the relatively short career of the student paraprofessional counselor.

Teamwork is essential in small, innovative programs, so it is necessary to address the issues inherent in professional-paraprofessional collegial relations. Peer counselors must learn how to use supervision, participate openly and equally in staff meetings, and benefit from consultation. Likewise, requisite professional skills are needed to provide timely and relevant supervision, solicit active student involvement in decision-making, and demonstrate by modeling and other behaviors the mutual process of giving and receiving consultation. It is also important to share informal events, thus improving personal as well as professional understanding by means of those humane and lighthearted personality attributes that may not be apparent or appropriate on the job.

Student Perspectives

Students should ultimately understand how and why they became involved and remained in a peer counseling or self-help program. In the recruitment phase, students may be referred to the program by a faculty member or another student. Through the initial interview they seek to understand the program goals and objectives in the light of their own interests and experience. They slowly become more attuned to the value of personal growth and the relationship between training and job performance. In the training phase they learn about such human development concepts as the need for autonomy among college-age students, the role of interpersonal relations, and the sorting out of life purposes that are facets of their own identity as well. While such concepts are applied to the student receiving services, they serve as personal signals for introspection by the peer helper as well. As a result, student trainees learn about goal setting, information and referral, and both helping and communication skills. Through experiential learning, especially role play, student paraprofessionals are evaluated for their suitability, oriented to their jobs, and become recipients of ongoing in-service training where the acquisition of specialized skills and personal development go hand in hand.

Professionals also need to acquire an understanding of the student perspective. Student paraprofessionals, like those in the community (Kahn, et al., 1981), frequently want to exercise fundamental control over their program activities, especially to facilitate the emergence of indigenous leadership and to build their own internal system of authority and responsibility. These dynamics require professionals to combine their wisdom and experience with significant respect for student culture and a belief in the ability of students to "get it together," especially during the early stages of program development. A positive and systematic training experience should encourage openness to additional, on-the-job learning and facilitate the development of trusting relationships with professionals. Such trust is frequently built upon the recognition that students actively need to articulate and demonstrate the values and culture of the campus student community in order to gain sufficient acceptance as a peer counselor or self-help organizer. Rich rewards for professionals who understand the student perspective come from observing the significant and rapid growth in self-confidence and sense of achievement. With strategic and sensitive guidance from professionals, student paraprofessionals are able to achieve significant personal growth and maturity from their program activities; testing career options is an unintended but frequent result for the students, as well.

Evaluation

The most difficult problem confronting campus peer counseling and self-help programs is the evaluation of their short-term and long-term impact on service recipients. This issue is related to a number of factors, but especially the nature of the programs and the current capabilities of evaluative research methodology. As with all human service programs, it is exceedingly difficult to select control groups of sufficient similarity and yet avoid the ethical dilemma of not serving or delaying service to someone of equal need for the sake of controlled research. Quasi-experimental designs are available for use in evaluating short-term outcomes of training or counseling, just as longitudinal time-series designs now exist for assessing long-term outcomes. Unfortunately, the human and financial resources needed to plan and implement innovative programs are so substantial as to preclude investing very much above the minimum in program evaluation. Model evaluation programs that require substantial investments might be more realistic than expecting every program to build in meaningful evaluation.

The methodological considerations are also important. For example, the outcomes of self-help programs do not easily fit with the few standardized instruments available to measure them. Second, most program evaluations are severely hampered by fluid changes in organizational life, which means that programs "don't stand still long enough to be measured." In essence, one is engaged in a quasi-photographic journey taking snap-shots of "moving targets" in an effort to capture the rich qualitative data inherent in dynamic programs. The evaluation, as a result, is usually characterized as a series of successive approximations without any of the actors "standing still and smiling."

Several evaluative activities are within the realm of possibility and need to receive more attention. These include methods for fairly rigorous pre- and posttest evaluations of training, for documenting periodic job performance evaluation, for evaluating the progress made in a single counseling case, and for costing out units of service as a method for evaluating the financial viability of programs. There are several useful program evaluation guides for assessing human service programs (Patton, 1978; Newman and Van Wijk, 1980).

An overriding goal of program evaluation is to inform decision making, whether it be progress made with a service recipient which is useful to the counselor or the value of training (Harvey & Passy, 1981) in relationship to job performance. Program managers need outcome and financial data in order to make necessary improvements and for dissemination to the campus community for purposes of credibility.

Further evaluation is needed to understand the possible causes of resistance to programs involving student paraprofessionals and the reasons for adequate faculty and administrative support for some programs but not others. Also, it will be important to evaluate different approaches to training, as well as the nature and scope of staff supervision required in different programs.

Conclusions

This analysis has highlighted several of the important issues for the planners and implementers of future peer counseling and self-help programs who need to give special attention to:

1. Defining need and program philosophy
2. Identifying both administrative and student perspectives
3. Planning for program evaluation at the outset

While some professionals have serious doubts about the capacity of student paraprofessional programs to survive on campuses

Epilogue: Implications for the Future

during this era of cutback management, it is unarguable that strong administrative support will be needed to sustain these important innovations. It is also important to identify other arenas in which to diffuse such creative programming, and two areas come to mind. First, since college innovations and discoveries are frequently translated into the culture of high schools and junior high schools (Gartner, et al., 1971), it might be worth exploring the utility of a broad range of peer counseling and self-help concepts and variables among the thirteen-eighteen year age-group. The value of students helping students should be clear and it seems relevant for younger students to acquire the skills of helping and organizing. Second, on a national level, many human service programs related to child abuse and neglect, foster care, mental health, juvenile justice, developmental disabilities, and substance abuse are experiencing a severe cutback in funding. In this context it seems relevant to explore the applicability of peer counseling and self-help strategies for empowering human service clients (Robin & Wagenfeld, 1981) and spreading the capacities of professional staff over an even wider domain than the traditional turf. Obviously, such ideas will require further experimentation and validation, hopefully carried out with the same vigor and creativity that we have witnessed on college campuses.

REFERENCES

Alley, S., Blanton, J., Feldman, R. E., Hunter, G. D., & Rofson, M. *Case studies of mental health paraprofessionals.* New York: Human Sciences Press, 1979.

Brown, W. F., & Delworth, U. Paraprofessionals: A member of the college guidance team. Chapter in Gartner, A., Riessman, F., & Jackson, V. C. (Eds.), *Paraprofessionals today. Volume I: Education.* New York: Human Sciences Press, 1977.

Delworth, U. Paraprofessionals as guerrillas: Recommendations for system change. *Personnel and Guidance Journal,* 1974, *53*(4), 335-338.

Ender, S. C., & McFadden, R. B. Training the student paraprofessional helper. Chapter 6 in Newton, F. B., & Ender, K. L. (Eds.), *Student development practices.* Springfield, Ill.: Charles C Thomas, Publisher, 1980.

Gartner, A., Kohler, M. C., & Riessman, F. *Children teach children: Learning by teaching.* New York: Harper & Row, 1971.

Gershon, M., & Biller, H. B. *The other helpers.* Lexington, Mass.: D. C. Heath, 1977.

Harvey, M. R., & Passy, L. E. A university-based new careers program. Section III in Robin, S. S., & Wagenfeld, M. O. (Eds.), *Paraprofessionals in the human services*. New York: Human Sciences Press, 1981.

Kahn, M. W., Henry, J., & Lejero, L. Indigenous mental health paraprofessionals on an Indian reservation. Section III in Robin, S. S., & Wagenfeld, M. O. (Eds.), *Paraprofessionals in the human services*. New York: Human Sciences Press, 1981.

Newman, H., & Van Wijk, A. *Self-evaluation for human service organizations*. New York: Greater New York Fund/United Way, 1980.

Patton, M. Q. *Utilization-focused evaluation*. Beverly Hills: Sage, 1978.

Pearl, A. Paraprofessionals and social change. *Personnel and Guidance Journal*, 1974, *53*(4), 264-268.

Robin, S. S. & Wagenfeld, M. O. (Eds.) *Paraprofessionals in the human services*. New York: Human Sciences Press, 1981.

Wagenfeld, M. O., & Robin, S. S. Reality, rhetoric and the paraprofessional: A concluding note. Section IV in Robin, S. S., & Wagenfeld, M. O. (Eds.), *Paraprofessionals in the human services*. New York: Human Sciences Press, 1981.

Warheit, G. J., Bell, R. A., & Schwab, J. J. *Needs assessment approaches: Concepts and methods*. Rockville, Md.: National Institute of Mental Health, 1977.

INDEX

A

AA (Alcoholics Anonymous), 5, 6, 58, 117
Academic credit for participation, 35, 84-85, 150
Accommodation in learning, 170, 171-73
Accountability, 73, 85
Administrative support, importance of, 174-75
Alteract (Project Alteract), 75-86, 132, 145, 155
APA (American Psychological Association), 16-17
APGA (American Personnel and Guidance Association), 16
"Aprofessional dimension, the," 7-8
Assessment, 12, 13
Assimilation in learning, 170, 171
Association of Retarded Citizens, 6

B

Bogust vs. Iverson, 156-57
Burnout, 32

C

Career
    choices, 165
    ladders (lattices), 14, 17, 179
Career Development Services, 143-47
Caring Community, the 116-128
CCIS (Curricular-Career Information Service), 43-53
College Students, 8, 14 (*see also* Paraprofessionals, Peer Counselors, and Volunteers)
Community agencies, backup for, 28
Community
    approaches to mental health, 86

feedback in planning, 77-78
    outreach, 29, 42, 105, 110, 124-26
Computers, 68-70, 83
Confidentiality, 134
Consultation, 131, 137, 180
Coordination of professional-paraprofessional team, 144-45
Cost-effectiveness, 13
Course credit (*see* Academic credit)
Counseling, by telephone, 27-42
Crisis intervention
    conditions for effective, 27
    in a drop-in center, 76, 78
    in drug abuse cases, 80
    through telephone counseling, 27-42

D

Daytop Village, 59, 63, 117, 118-19
DISC House (Drug Information and Service Center), 55-59, 62
DISC Village, 59-62, 117

E

Evaluation, 10-15, 50, 181-82
    forms of, 40
    of Curricular-Career Information Service, 50
    of drop-in and outreach center, 85
    of paraprofessional academic advising, 7-71
    of paraprofessional administrative aide program, 148-49
    of women's self-help group program, 101-02

F

Faculty, 126-27, 177
Florida State University Counseling Center, 27, 30, 91, 94, 105, 130, 143, 145

Funding, 47, 72, 114, 149-50, 183
Future implications of paraprofessional-ism, 15-17

G
Gay
    peer counseling service, 105, 106, 110-13, 114
    rap group, 105, 106-09, 113, 114
Gay Liberation Front, 105
Glasser, William, 54, 55-56, 58, 117-18 127
Group leaders training program, 119, 120, 124
Groups
    encounter, 122-23
    format to accelerate movement in, 94-99
    growth, 81-82
    human potential, 119, 126
    intensive growth, 131
    marathon, 122
    problems with open membership in, 109
    voluntary involvement in, 122-24
    women's self-help, 91-102

H
Human potential movement, 119, 123
Human relations training, 76, 78

J
Job descriptions, 179

L
Legal responsibility, 156-159, 160

M
McBride vs. State, 157-58, 159
Manpower
    effect of limited funding on, 149
    mix in an administrative team, 143-45
    ratio of professionals to nonprofes-sionals, 28-30, 46, 76, 93, 165-66
Methodological consciousness, 168, 172
Minority Student Affairs, 146-47

N
Needs assessment techniques, 177

O
Off-Campus Student Association, 82, 85, 132

P
Paraprofessional
    academic advising program, 65-68
    administrative program goals, 148
    counseling, 13, 55
    professional relations, 179
    salaries, 144, 149-50
    staff growth experiences, 82
    perspectives on own involvement, 180
    training issues, 175
Paraprofessionalism, future implications of, 15-17
Paraprofessionals
    advantages of, 70
    as academic advisors, 68, 69, 70
    as drug center staff, 56-58
    as liaison between students and profes-sionals, 148
    as models, 98
    as program designers, 132
    as program planners, 135-36
    as trainers, 132, 145
    as women's group leaders, 93, 95, 97-99
    conditions for use of, 52
    distrust of, 149
    drawbacks of, 8, 70-71, 149
    evaluation of performance of, 51
    history of, 4-5
    in administration, 143-50
    legal liability of, 160
    motivation of, 132-33, 135
    recruitment of, 72-73, 84
    resistance to, 182
    roles of, 9-10
    selection of, 99, 130, 143-44
    supervision of, 99-100, 158-59, 179-80
    training of, 47-49, 66, 69-70, 73, 132, 175
    (see also Peer counselors)
Parents Without Partners, 6
Participatory Management, 178
Peer counseling
    approach to drug counseling, 63
    effectiveness, 17

possibilities on Asian campuses, 164-65
selection in, 176
services, need for, 176
training in high school, 125
training program as community outreach, 125
Peer counseling programs, 3, 13, 175
Peer counselors
as academic advisors, 70, 86, 177
as program planners, 76-77
desirable characteristics for, 14
disadvantages of, 15
gay, 105, 106, 110-13
in the student Caring Community, 118, 119
paraprofessionals as trainers of, 132, 140
perspectives on own involvement, 180
resident assistants, 43, 47-48, 50, 51
(see also Paraprofessionals)
Peer supervision of paraprofessional group leaders, 100-01
Phoenix House, 59
Planning and organization, 12
Problem identification in advisement, 43-46
Professionalism, 16-17
Professionals
and paraprofessionals, distinctions between, 9
legal responsibility of, 156-59
paraprofessional relations, 31, 106, 179, 180
selection of suitable, 12
Program
development, 86, 93
evaluation (see Evaluation)
impact, 10-15
management, 178
philosophy, 177-78
Public education efforts, 82
Publicity, 77, 84, 94, 105-06

R
Reality Therapy, 55-58, 117, 127
Recruitment, 31
of group members, 94
of volunteers for community action, 82

Replication, 72
Resident Assistants (RAs), 43, 47-48, 50, 51
Role play, 33, 36-40, 137-139, 150, 171

S
Salary, 149
Scare wheel, 133, 135
Scheduling, 32-33
Selection, 12, 130
as a determinant of program success, 176
as personnel management, 178
of members of Caring Community, 121-22
of paraprofessional academic advisors, 69
of paraprofessional administrative aides, 143-44
process inadequacies, 150
Self-help
characteristics of, 6
effectiveness of, 17
movement, 3-6, 8
programs in relation to university structure, 175
services, need for, 176
strategies, 183
Self-help groups
assessment of, 13
counseling style, 17
processes of, 6-7
women's, 17, 91-102
Social action, gay, 109
Social Action Projects (SAPS), 76, 82-84
Social group work method, 105, 108
Staffing, 131
State University of New York at Purchase, 117
Student problems in Asian universities, 163-64
Student volunteers (see Peer Counselors, Paraprofessionals)
Synanon, 6, 117

T
Tallahassee Memorial Hospital, 80
Teamwork, 179
Telephone Counseling Service (TCS), 27-

42, 106, 132, 155

Trainers
  interaction with trainees, 137-141
  selection of, 132

Training, 12, 28, 77
  format for Telephone Counseling Service, 33-40
  issues, 175
  of Caring Community group leaders, 123
  of faculty academic advisors, 66
  of gay peer counselors, 106, 110-11
  of paraprofessional academic advisors, 66, 69-70, 73
  of paraprofessionals, 47-49, 175
  of peer counselors in drop-in center, 79-80
  of student counselors for overseas education programs, 130-41

  opportunities for students, 30
  role playing in, 33-40, 137
  use of anxiety in, 141

V
Volunteers
  as faculty academic advisors, 66-67
  as primary manpower, 28-29
  course credit for, 35
  recruitment, selection and training of, 31-40
  supervision of, 159
  (see also Paraprofessionals and Peer Counselors)

W
Widow-to-Widow, 6
Women
  in gay peer counseling program, 113
  in self-help groups, 91-102